THE TECHNIQUE OF
BRUGES FLOWER
LACE

THE TECHNIQUE OF
BRUGES FLOWER LACE

Veronica Sorenson and
J. Rombach-de Kievid

B.T. Batsford Ltd • London

First published 1995
Reprinted 1996

Typeset by Servis Filmsetting Ltd, Manchester
and printed in Great Britain by
The Bath Press, Bath

Published by
B.T. Batsford Ltd
4 Fitzhardinge Street
London W1H 0AH

A catalogue record for this book is available from the
British Library

ISBN 0 7134 7329 0

Thanks to Judy Hemstead and Norma Hanstead for
proof reading and correcting my mistakes. Also to
Dick Chenery for his photographic expertise and
Puck Smelter-Hoekstra and Johanna Giesen for the
translation of the original Dutch script.

Every piece of lace (except that shown in photograph
45c) was made by Veronica Sorenson. Prickings
numbered 9, 10, 11, 12, 13, 14, 15, 17, 18, 19, 20, 21,
23, 24, 29, 31, 34, 35, 36, 37, 40, 41, 42, 43, 46 were
designed by J. Rombach de-Kievid. All the others
were designed by Veronica Sorenson.

Contents

Introduction

Bruges Flower lace originates in Bruges, Belgium, and is characterised by its own unique techniques. Designs consist of many different flowers, leaves and braids forming loops and scrolls, and in this volume we will be describing the most common.

Each technical aspect of this lace is explained fully and will be found under separate headings e.g. Scrolls, Sewings, False Plaits. For greater clarity, the text is accompanied by diagrams which show the position of each thread although, occasionally, schematic drawings are used. These consist of continuous lines where each line represents a pair of threads. This is particularly helpful when discussing leaves.

The majority of the designs require BOUC 50/2, Bockens 40/2 or Campbells 70/2 linen thread. It is advisable to use linen thread when the lace is to be mounted on linen material and cotton thread for mounting on cotton material. The equivalent cotton thread used is DMC 60 Cordonnet. Try to avoid mixing linen and cotton threads in one design.

Although the above threads are all approximately the same thickness, it is essential to work a sample piece before making the actual design as every make of thread is of a slightly different thickness (even different batches of the same thread have been known to be so) and it may be necessary to add or subtract a pair of passives to obtain the best results.

Prickings for the various elements of Bruges Flower lace i.e. individual flowers, leaves and braids are included for practice and we hope that lacemakers using this volume will be able to create new designs of their own with the assistance of these. Any pricking requiring a thread of different thickness to those mentioned above will clearly state this.

There are many uses for Bruges Flower lace. Single motifs can be used to decorate a pocket, purse, tie, teacosy, pillow corner or lampshade. Single flowers look lovely decorating cushions and tablecloths for garden use, for example. Edgings may be used around tablecloths, pillow slips, sleeves, skirts, lampshades and necklines.

All-lace mats are attractive objects in their own right but they can also be used to decorate a cushion cover or used as a window hanging. Many all-lace mats have details which stand as motifs on their own. And what about collars and cuffs, fans, crosses and even 3-D pictures? The list of uses is almost endless and some of them are examined later on in this book.

1
Stitches

Lace stitches can be made in two different ways – namely the 'open' method and the 'closed' method. When using the open method, the stitch is commenced with a 'twist'. The closed method ends with the twist. Regardless of the method used, the finished lace will look the same. It is essential, though, that the same method is used throughout any one pattern.

English lacemakers not familiar with continental phraseology and methods normally use the closed method of working. In English terminology, a 'cross' means two over three. A twist consists of the moves two over one and four over three, worked at the same time.

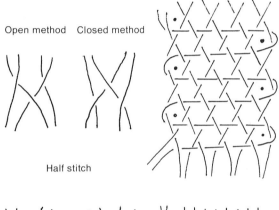

Open method   Closed method

Half stitch

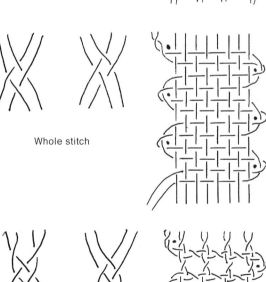

Whole stitch

Whole stitch and twist

Diag. 1 *Stitches used in Bruges Flower lace*

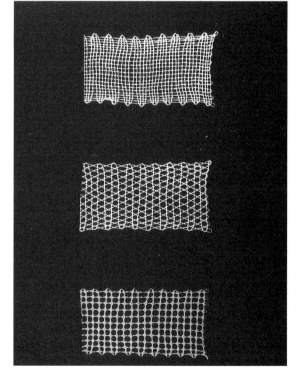

Top – whole stitch   Centre – half stitch
Bottom – whole stitch and twist

8

2
Braids

Whole stitch braid

The braid for Bruges Flower Lace is worked either in whole stitch with the first and last passive pairs in whole stitch and twist; or in half stitch but still working the first and last passives in whole stitch and twist.

The worker pair is the one which runs horizontally through the work whilst the passive pairs are the vertical threads.

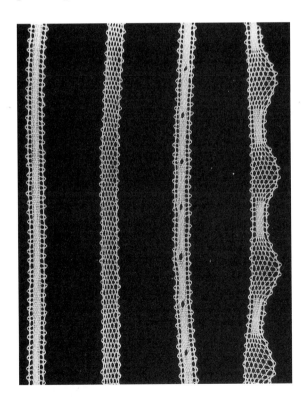

Braid samples

Pricking 1 *Practice prickings for braids*

Braids in whole and half stitch

Braids can also be worked in alternate blocks of whole stitch and half stitch separated by a row of whole stitch. This latter row is always worked from the outer edge to the inner one. The half-stitch sections are often worked round a curve which widens and then returns to its original width when whole stitch is worked again. For clarity, the sample is worked straight.

Braids with small eyelet holes

In slightly wider braids a decorative hole can be worked. An odd number of passive pairs is needed to work this. The worker travels to the centre of the braid (but does not work through the central passive pair) and is left to become a passive. The unworked middle passive pair is then used to continue that row as a worker pair and remains the worker until the next hole is made. It is permissible to use a support pin to prevent the work becoming uneven in the centre of the braid.

Curves in braids

If the pattern shows more pin holes on the outside of a curve than on the inside, it is necessary to use each inner pin more than once. This is known either as 'working the pin twice' or working a 'pivot pin'.

Working the pin twice – Pin A on *diagram 2(i)* is shown as two separate pinholes for clarity, although it is, in fact, only one. The first time it is used it is worked normally but the second time the workers do not make a stitch with the last passive pair. They merely twist twice and pass over the last passive and round the back of the pin (the pin is not removed). Then they work a whole stitch and twist with the outer passive pair and the next row is continued.

Sharp bends – If the bend is sharp, pin A on *diagram 2(ii)* is worked a number of times. The diagram shows it opened up as before, demonstrating that each time the pin is used the workers are twisted twice but do not make a stitch with the last passive pair at all but pass over it; round the pin with two twists; then under it as shown. This is repeated as necessary until the pricking indicates that the worker travels to the next pin in the braid. The pivot pin is then removed and the unworked passive pair eased slightly to make a smooth edge.

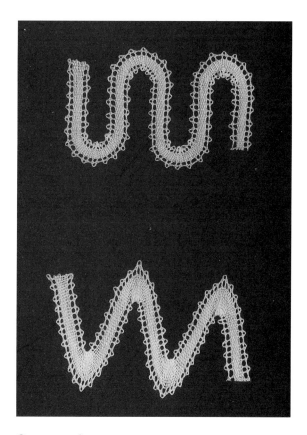

Curve samples

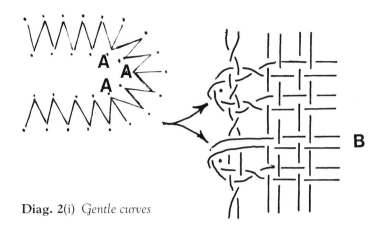

Diag. 2(i) *Gentle curves*

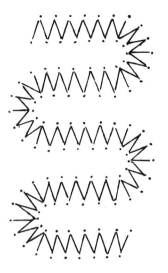

Pricking 2(i)
Practice pricking for gentle curves

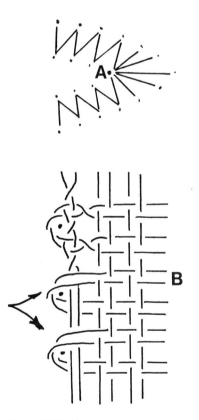

Diag. 2(ii) *Sharp curves*

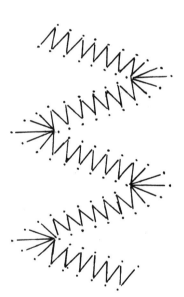

Pricking 2(ii)
Practice pricking for sharp curves

11

Braids beginning with a scroll

There are two methods of working a scroll. The first one described here is best used when the braid is a narrow one. The second method is preferred for a wider braid which entails adding in a larger number of passives.

Method 1

Put a thick pin in the larger dot shown on the pricking as in *diagram 3(i)*. Hang four pairs on this pin (*diagram 3(ii)*) and twist the inner pair five times. Lay a long loop of spare thread round the twisted pair as shown and leave it to the back. This thread may be omitted as it is only included to help complete the sewing at the end of the scroll.

The worker is the second pair from the left and the braid is worked in whole stitch with the last pair to the right in whole stitch and twist. The left-hand passive pair next to the thick pin is used for the pivot as in the method of working sharp curves shown in *diagram 3(iii)* (each line represents a pair). The finished scroll is shown in *photograph 4(A)*.

Adding extra passives – As the braid widens, extra passive pairs are required. Put a support pin either between two threads in the work or a little to the rear of the work. Hang the new pair on it and lay the threads either side of a 'top' thread as shown in *diagram 3(iv)*. After working a few rows, the support pin is removed and the new passive pair is eased down into position. This movement is repeated until there are enough passives in the braid.

Completing the scroll – When pin A on *diagram 3(i)* has been worked, the thick pivot pin is removed and the left-hand passive pair (the one that has not been worked) is sewn into the lowest loop at the beginning of the scroll. This is where the spare loop of thread is useful to pull one passive thread through instead of using a crochet hook. The braid is now continued; work the pivotal passives in whole stitch and twist.

Method 2

This is basically the same as Method 1 except for the commencement and the sewing. Four pairs are hung on as in *diagram 3(ii)* but the outer pair is twisted five times and the inner pair three times. The worker is then the left-hand pair. When the scroll has been completed and the thick pin removed, the pivotal passive pair is still sewn into the beginning, but this is easier to do with a crochet hook due to the extra twists, and the loop of thread may not be required. The finished scroll is shown in the photograph.

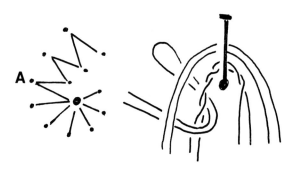

(i) *The pricking*   (ii) *Hanging on pairs*

(iii) *Working the pivot*

(iv) *Adding extra passives*

Diag. 3 *Starting a braid with a scroll*

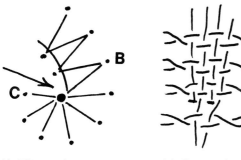

(i) *The pricking* (ii) *Losing threads* (iii) *The final row of working – method 1* (iv) *The final row of working – method 2*

Diag. 4 *Finishing a braid with a scroll*

Braids ending with a scroll

Method 1

The method used for this is almost a reverse of the scroll beginning (*diagram 4(i)*). The pivot operation is commenced after pin B has been worked. As the braid narrows passive pairs are discarded. Avoid losing two adjacent threads and try to make sure that it is 'top' threads that are discarded (*diagram 4(ii)*).

Continue to discard passive pairs until a total of three passives and the worker are left and pin C on *diagram 4(i)* is reached. Work back towards the pivot pin as in *diagram 4(iii)* by working one whole stitch and twist and then one whole stitch. Tie pairs 1 and 4 over the top of 2 and 3. Then remove the thick pin and sew the worker (pair 2) into the bottom of the pile of loops. Now tie the worker and pair 3 together. An extra loop of thread as at the beginning of the scroll may be used here. The finished scroll is shown in *photograph 4(C)*.

Method 2

Work the scroll as for Method 1 until pin C is reached. The worker now travels back to the pivot pin and out again, as if there is another outer pin to work, and left there (*diagram 4(iv)*).

The pivot pin is now removed and the centre pivotal passive pair is sewn into the loop at the bottom of the pile. Now the other two passive pairs and lastly the worker are all sewn separately into the same hole. The threads are then tied and cut. The finished scroll is shown in *photograph 4(D)*.

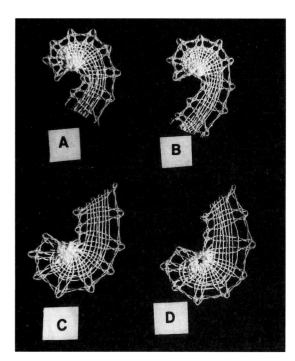

Scrolls (A) *commencement method 1*
(B) *commencement method 2*
(C) *finish method 1*
(D) *finish method 2*
Enlargements all shown on the wrong side

13

Crossing braids

When braids cross one another, the braid underneath is worked first. See *diagram 5* – Braid 1. As Braid 2 reaches the crossing point, the workers are sewn in at points A and B by removing the pin already worked for Braid 1 and replacing it after the sewing has been worked.

The worker pair then travels from B to C by working across all the passives and sewings are worked in a like manner at C and D before continuing Braid 2.

If the braids are wide there are more rows of work within the area of the crossing and these must be worked for *both* braids (not just the underneath one) to prevent untidy work.

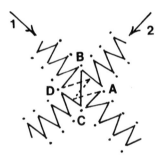

Diag. 5 *Crossing braids*

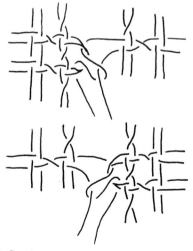

Diag. 6 *Sewings*

Sewings for the crossings

These are simple sewings of one pair using a crochet hook. After removing the pin, a loop of thread from one of the workers is pulled through the existing hole. The other worker thread is passed through this loop; the threads are then tightened and the pin replaced (*diagram 6*).

The five small braid samples in *pricking 3* offer practice in scrolls, crossing braids and sewings.

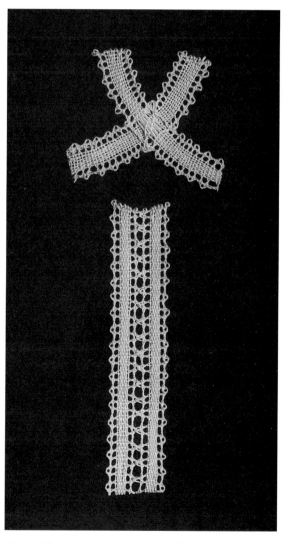

Crossed braids showing reverse side and sample of braids joined with sewings

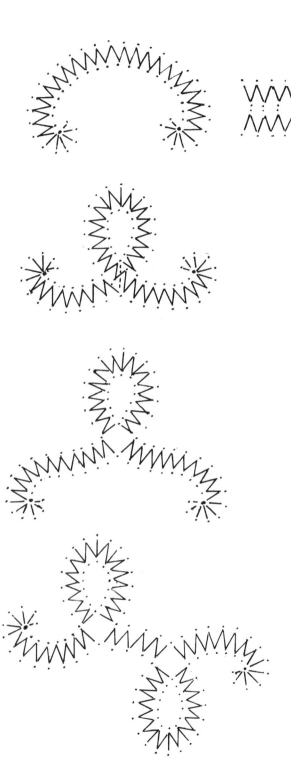

Pricking 3 *Samples of scrolls and crossed braids including sewings*

Scrolls and crossed braids

Commencing a braid from the side of another

In this type of lace a pricking often indicates that a braid is required which starts at the side of one already worked or even from a flower or leaf. The pairs for the new braid are sewn in to the existing lace. They can be hung either from a pin hole or on the twisted outer passive threads.

To hang in a pin hole, remove the pin and pull a loop of the new pair through the resultant hole (*diagram 7(i)*). One end of the new pair is passed through this loop (*diagram 7(ii)*) and the threads tightened neatly. A similar movement is made for hanging the new pair on the twisted passives between the pin holes.

Sometimes it is necessary to attach two pairs at one pin hole. When this is required an alternative method is used which does not result in a small knot of thread. Wind only one bobbin of each new pair leaving a length of thread and pull the end of that thread right through the loop of the original lace. The second bobbins of the new pairs can now be wound (*diagram 7(iii and iv)*).

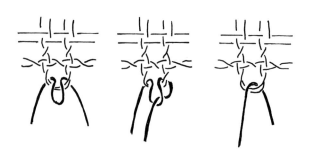

Diag. 7 *Hanging in new braid threads from lace already made*

Commencing a braid at a slant to another

When the new braid is at a slant from the original braid or flower petal, the method is slightly different and the second method of hanging in pairs is preferred, so that the first rows of work are smooth.

When all the new pairs have been hung on, the first row of work does not travel all the way across the new braid, but just as far as the centre and then returns to the side before working across all the passives for the third row of work.

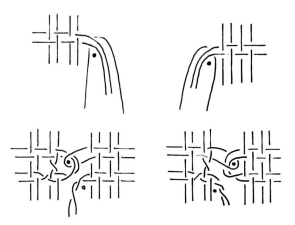

Diag. 8 *Method of dividing braids and adding extra worker pair*

Dividing braids

A pattern sometimes indicates that a wide braid divides into two narrower ones. Work as far as the dividing pin. Now divide the passives equally into two and put the dividing pin between them. A new worker pair is first hung on the dividing pin and the original worker passes to the back of this pin; round it; and then under one thread of the new pair (*diagram 8(i and ii)*). The workers have come from the left side.

The new worker is used for the right-hand part of the divided braid and the original one for the left side. When the workers come from the right side, this movement is reversed (*diagram 8(iii and iv)*).

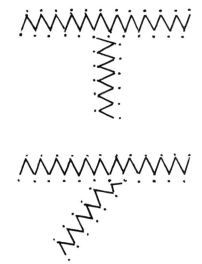

Pricking 4 *Practice prickings for commencing a braid from the side of another and dividing braids*

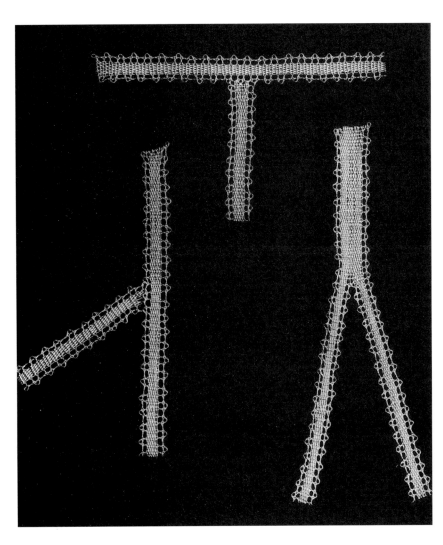

Commencing new braids and dividing braids

3
Flowers

The flowers in Bruges Flower lace are varied and can be circular or oval but they are always full-faced and not depicted sideways. They consist of two separate parts – the petals and a filling in the centre, sometimes with a ring of braid separating the two.

There are usually six or eight petals which are worked alternately in whole stitch and half stitch but (as in braids) the first and last passives are always worked as whole stitch and twist.

Bruges Flower lace flowers

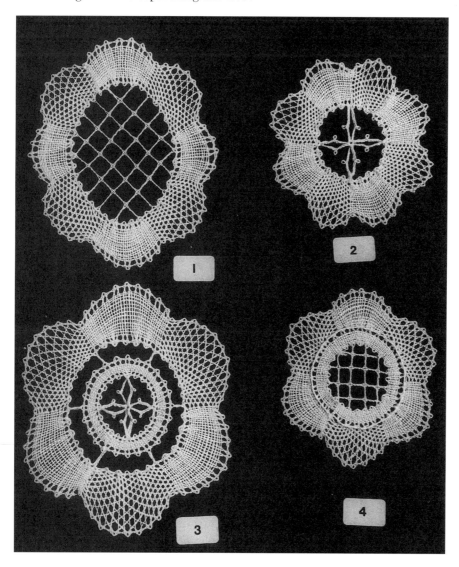

Pricking 5 *Pricking for four flower samples*

The petals

The narrowest line of work between the petals is worked from the outside to inside, usually in whole stitch and twist (see arrows on *diagram 9*).

The pin holes on the outer edge of the petals are often fewer than those on the inner edge. The inner pins are then worked twice in the same fashion as the inner pins on braid curves. Sometimes every inner pin is used in this way. Flowers can also have their passives plaited between each petal for a more open decorative effect.

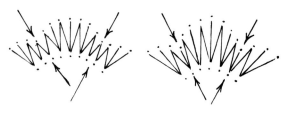

Diag. 9 *Flower petals – starting places*

When looking at a pattern, the first problem is to know where to start. The best place is that which provides the least visible ending. In this type of lace the division between the flower petals provides the best place as the ends are joined to the starting loops.

To start a petal
The first petal to work will be a whole stitch one. Hang the pairs on a row of pins directly above or on the first line of work. The knots from the end sewing will then lie on top of the block of whole stitch.

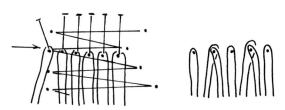

Diag. 10 *Starting a Bruges Flower*

The workers are hung on the edge dot to the left. See *diagram 10(i)* and the passives on a row of pins in the v-shape to the pattern. If there is not sufficient space for a pin for each passive pair, two pairs may be hung on a pin, laying them side by side so that there are two separate loops when the pin is removed (*diagram 10(ii)*).

Note When working the 'open' method, the pairs should all be crossed before working. Although the twists are lost when the pins are removed, the loops are fractionally larger thus assisting the end sewings. Note also that these instructions are for flowers worked in a clockwise direction. Many English lacemakers will discover that their general practice of working the foot to the right side of the work will make them want to work the flower in an anticlockwise direction and use the 'closed' method. This is equally acceptable but remember to make allowances for this when following instructions as some may need reversing.

Finishing the petals
The last row of the petals will be a row of whole stitch just above the start. Before sewing in each pair, twist it once and pull a loop of the left thread through the start loop, as in *diagram 11(i and ii)*. Now the right-hand thread of the pair is threaded through the loop of the left-hand thread and the threads tightened. When working braids in the flower centres, they are all in whole stitch so do not twist before the sewing (*diagram 11(iii)*). When each pair is sewn in the threads can be tied in the manner of the Bruges method.

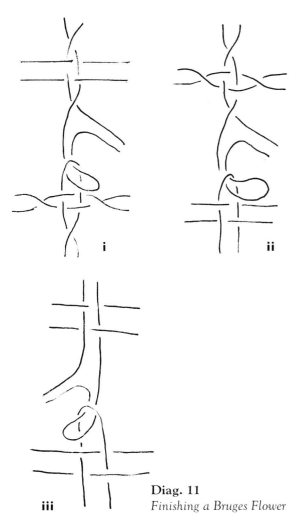

Diag. 11
Finishing a Bruges Flower

thread and make another half knot with the left thread and the next one to the right (*diagram 12(ii)*), and so on along the row. The right-hand thread must be on top of the left-hand one as you start the half knot. By working this way, the knots are all pulled towards the worker as shown in *diagram 12(iii)*.

Second row of knots: (right to left) The left-hand thread must be on top of the right-hand one for each knot as in *diagram 12(iv)*, working in reverse to the first row. After each half knot, leave the left-hand thread and work the next knot with the right-hand thread and the next one (*diagram 12(v)*). The knots all face downwards as shown in *diagram 12(vi)*. The last pair is tied a second time and the threads can be cut short.

Note This method of tying the threads is only suitable when joining petals of a flower or a braid. It should not be used, for example, when joining areas of Torchon ground or other open work.

Tying the threads: the Bruges method

When the petals are finished the worker is to the right, so commence the tying at the left so that the worker at the other end can be pulled a little tighter to make a neater join. The knots are formed by tying the threads in two rows. If the worker is at the left side of the work, the second row is worked first, then the first row and the very last knot is made with an extra half knot.

First row of knots: (left to right) commence with the first two threads and make a half knot (*diagram 12(i)*). Leave the right-hand

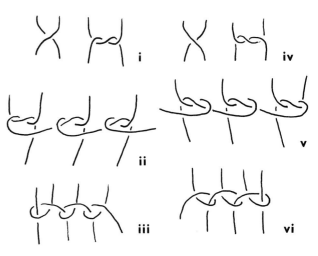

Diag. 12 *The Bruges method of tying threads*

Flower centres

There are a number of variations in the fillings for flower centres. They can be roughly divided as follows:
1 Torchon ground.
2 Plait and picot filling.
3 Plain plaits.
4 A filling and separate braid with false plaits between the braid and petals.
5 A filling stitch enclosed by a braid which has a raised vein at the inner petal edge.

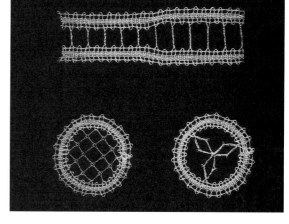

Practice pieces for flower centres and false plaits

Flower 1

This flower has a Torchon filling. After working the petals for this flower the centre has a filling commonly called Torchon ground. Hang the number of pairs required at the pinholes of the inner edge of the petals. Work half stitch, pin, half stitch at each pin and twist the pairs as often as necessary to provide a firm ground between each pin (*diagram 13*).

On the small practice filling *pricking 6(a)*, two pairs are hung at A. At B and C the pairs are sewn in and carry on to work down to D. When the entire filling is completed and the pairs all sewn in, tie and cut the threads.

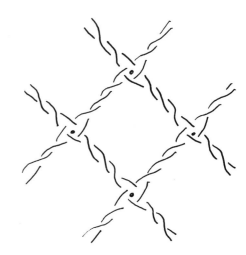

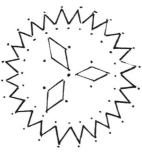

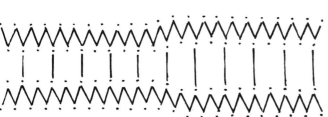

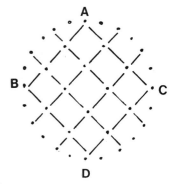

Diag. 13
Flower 1 – filling (Torchon ground)

Pricking 6 *Practice pricking for flower centres and false plaits*

Flower 2

This flower has a plait and picot filling. For lacemakers not familiar with this technique the plait with picots is worked as follows:

Plait This requires two pairs of bobbins. A whole stitch is worked to commence it i.e. cross, twist, cross. It is continued by working twists and crosses alternately (*diagram 14(i)*). Tighten the threads after each 'cross' to make the plait firm by easing each pair into position. Always end the plait with a 'cross'.

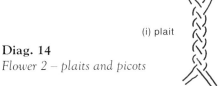

(i) plait

Diag. 14
Flower 2 – plaits and picots

Picots Two different methods of working picots can be used in Bruges Flower lace. The first method is ideal for fillings, but when a plait and picot border is worked it is better to use the second method of double picots, to make a stronger finish. It is not advisable merely to wind a single thread round a pin as a picot. The picots for fillings are single ones but the thread is knotted to retain its position. Use one of the pairs of the plait. For a picot on the right, the right-hand pair is used. A right-hand picot is worked thus:

(ii) right-hand picot

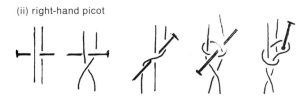

Left-hand picots use the left hand pair of the plait thus:

(iii) left-hand picot

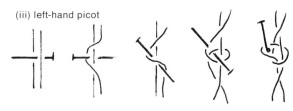

Double picots are worked as shown below:

left-hand picot

(iv) left-hand double picot

right-hand picot

(v) right-hand double picot

The centre of Flower 2 is worked using two pairs of bobbins taken from the petals while they are still being worked. The inside passive and the worker pairs are used commencing from the last place where the filling touches the petals.

Put a pin between the two pairs at the start of the plait (*diagram 15(i)*). The filling is worked in the sequence shown in *diagram 15(ii)*. The centre pin is put between the plait pairs and the left-hand pair is twisted once to make a hole for the sewing. The plait is sewn in to the inner line of petals as shown in *diagram 15(iii)* using the nearest pair from the plait. It is possible to use both pairs as in *diagram 15(iv)* for the sewing, but the join is then thicker. The centre plaits are all sewn together the last time the plaits reach it.

When the filling is complete, sew the pairs back into the pinhole on the petal edge and continue making the petal as before.

Work the centre braid as far as the first pin, which indicates it needs to be joined to the petals, and work a false plait.

False Plaits   Twist the workers as many times as necessary to make a firm twist and sew into the pinhole as in *diagram 16(i)*. Now twist them twice and sew them over the original twists (*diagram 16(ii)*). Twist them once more and sew in again if it is a long false plait. End by twisting them one more time after the last sewing.

Now continue the braid beginning with whole stitch and twist until the last point of contact with the inner plaits and picot filling. Work this and then complete the centre braid.

If the centre filling is Torchon ground, follow the instructions for Flower 1 centre filling.

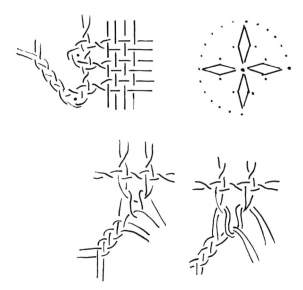

Diag. 15
Flower 2 – plait and picot filling and sewing

Flower 3

The centre of this flower has a separate braid which is joined to the petals with false plaits. The inner filling is the same as in Flower 2. Once again, the petals are worked first, ready for joining in the false plaits.

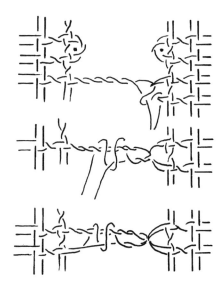

Diag. 16 *Flower 3 – false plaits*

Flower 4

The centre filling of this flower has a braid joined directly to the petals with raised sewings to form a vein where they meet. This flower is the exception to the rule that the petals are always worked first, because the braid must be completed before the rest of the flower. The braid has a straight footside on the outside edge with the petals sewn over this edge to make the vein, which is in the form of a raised line on the right side of the work.

To start the straight edge Hang two worker pairs at the beginning, as in *diagram 17(i)* and work a half stitch with them. The left-hand pair will be the first worker. Twist it twice (*diagram 17(ii)*) before using it. The right-hand pair becomes the second worker. Twist it twice to form the outer edge. The inner edge is plain, i.e. the last passive pair is worked in wholestitch, the workers twisted twice around the pin, which is then covered in whole stitch.

To work the straight edge When the worker reaches the right-hand side, make a whole stitch and twist with the other worker but put the pin inside both pairs as in *diagram 17(iii)*. The left-hand pair is now the new worker. Twist both pairs twice before continuing.

Work the complete braid and then the centre filling. If that is Torchon ground, work it as in Flower 1. If it is a plait and picot filling (as in Flower 2) it is made when the last point of contact is reached. Then the braid can be finished.

The petals are now worked, making raised sewings at the inner pin holes where the straight edge was made for the braid.

Raised sewings can be made either from a block of whole stitch or of half stitch and can also be worked from the left or right. A raised sewing is made as follows (*diagram 18*): remove the pin, twist the worker pair once before doing the sewing and make the sewing across both loops as illustrated. The petal can now be continued. It may not be necessary to replace the pin.

If the pattern shows that there must be two separate raised sewings into the loop, use only the upper loop for the first sewing and the lower loop for the second (*diagram 18 (v and vi)*). The pin is replaced after each sewing to keep the vein straight.

Diag. 17
Flower 4 – starting braid with straight edge

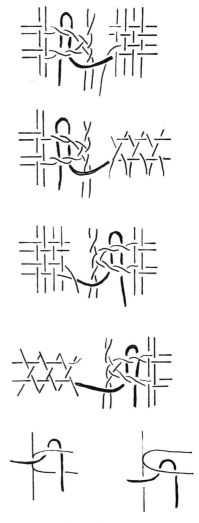

Diag. 18 *Flower 4 – raised sewings*

4
Leaves

There are three main leaf shapes in Bruges Flower lace, and each shape can be worked in two different ways. They are formed either working straight from the tip to the base with an openwork vein in the centre, or by working up one side and down the other with the choice of a raised vein or open vein in the centre. The different shapes can be identified by the terms 'single leaf', 'double leaf' and 'triple leaf'.

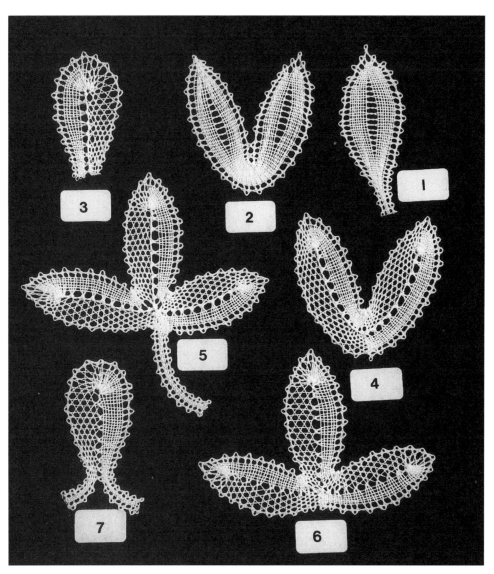

Bruges Flower lace leaves

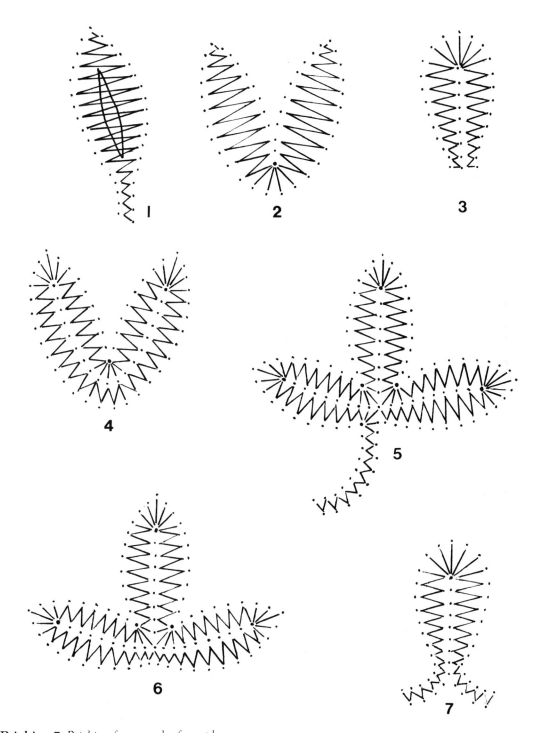

Pricking 7 *Pricking for seven leaf samples*

Leaf 1 (single leaf)

This is worked from the tip to the base. Referring to *diagram 19(i)*, hang two pairs at the tip as shown and work a whole stitch and twist with them. These two pairs form either side of the edge of the leaf and are worked in whole stitch and twist.

Hang two more pairs on each of the pin holes 2, 3, 4 and 5 on *diagram 19(ii)*. Using the pairs from pin 1, work whole stitch and twist through them on both sides. Now the right hand pair from 2 works whole stitch through the three pairs to the left and stays there. With the left hand pair from 3, work whole stitch through the five pairs to the right and leave them there. The right-hand pair from 4 works whole stitches through seven pairs to the left and so on until there are sufficient pairs to fill the centre. Now work as usual in whole stitch, twisting the outside pairs.

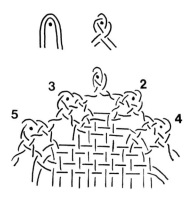

Diag. 19 *Starting a single leaf*

Open vein As the leaf widens an open vein can be made by twisting the worker pair once or twice in the centre. As the leaf narrows at its foot, passives must be discarded. The base of the leaf is either continued as a braid or the remaining pairs can be sewn in to part of the lace already made.

Leaf 2 (double leaf)

A double leaf commences in the same way as a single one. Start at point A on *diagram 20* and work an open vein where necessary. At the join of the two leaves pin B is worked as a pivot pin in the same way as for a sharp bend.

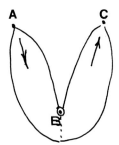

Diag. 20 *Double leaf – direction of work*

Discard threads as the tip of the second leaf is neared and when this point is reached at pin C and has been worked, turn the pillow round and plait the remaining four pairs back over the whole stitch of the leaf and sew them down over it, using two of the discarded threads to hold them in place.

If the pattern indicates that a plait from a filling touches the tip of the second leaf, the last two pairs can be used for that.

Note A double leaf can also be worked by treating it as two single leaves. Tie the threads from each together where they meet in a reef knot and then in two rows using the Bruges method of finishing.

Leaves with raised veins

These are not difficult but present a different aspect to those already described. Both types of leaf have the outside edge passives worked as whole stitch and twist, but these leaves are started at the base and worked up one side in whole stitch and back down the other in half stitch. As the whole stitch part is worked, a straight edge is formed with two alternate workers along the centre. The second, half stitch part of the leaf is joined to the first with raised sewings.

Leaf 3
(single leaf with raised vein)

This can be started either by hanging pairs in from part of the design already worked or as a continuation of a braid (*diagram 21(i and ii)*). It may be necessary to add more pairs as the leaf widens and to discard them in the second side of the leaf as it narrows. Adding in extra threads is done as previously described for starting a braid with a scroll.

Commence the leaf where indicated on *diagram 21* and, following the arrows, work in whole stitch with a straight edge at the centre. The top inside pin hole is worked as a pivot pin. Change to half stitch at the tip and work back down with raised sewings at the central straight edge.

When taking out pairs from a half stitch area, always use edge pairs not centre ones:

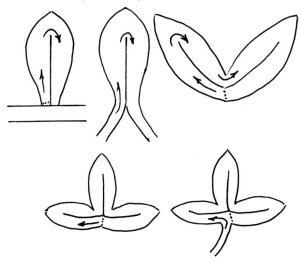

Diag. 21 *Direction of work for leaves with raised veins*

using centre pairs causes untidiness in the structure of half stitch. To lose threads in half stitch, work a complete row to the outside of the leaf. Put in the pin and (leaving the workers outside the pin) work a half stitch with the first two passive pairs as shown in *diagram 22*. Take out the right hand thread of each of these pairs and tie them. Now, twist the remaining two threads once and work one whole stitch and twist with the workers and then work back across the row in half stitch.

Diag. 22 *Discarding pairs in half stitch*

Leaf 4
(double leaf with raised vein)

Start where indicated and follow the arrows on *diagram 21(iii)*, working straight edges at the centre as before.

Leaf 5
(triple leaf with raised vein)

This is an extension of the double leaf and is worked in the same manner.

Note Leaves can also be worked without the central raised vein, by ignoring the second worker pair and working the centre pin without twisting the end passives of the row. This forms a flat row of small holes as the half stitch side is worked with normal sewings, rather than the raised line of twisted thread. Leaves 6 and 7 in the photograph at the start of this chapter are worked in this manner.

5
Joining motifs, filling spaces and edgings

As Bruges Flower lace is a sectional lace rather than a continuous one, it needs to have its various component parts joined together. This can be done in a number of different ways.

1 The parts can be joined together during the working with sewings as in *diagram 6* (simple sewings).
2 They may be joined with a false plait as in *diagram 16*.
3 They can be connected with a plait and picot shape when the area is too large for either of the above. This is similar to the centre filling for Flower 2.
4 Very large spaces can be filled in many ways e.g.
   a Torchon ground with extra twists.
   b Hexagonal filling of plaits and false plaits.

c Plait and picot fillings.
d Plain plaits which cross with 'windmills' (four-pair crossings).
e Plaits which cross leaving an area of half stitch (known as 'Bedfordshire spiders' or 'Snowflake' ground in England).

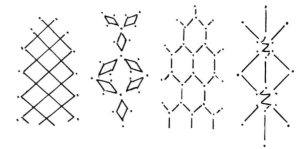

Diag. 23 *Filling stitches for large spaces*

Fillings for large spaces

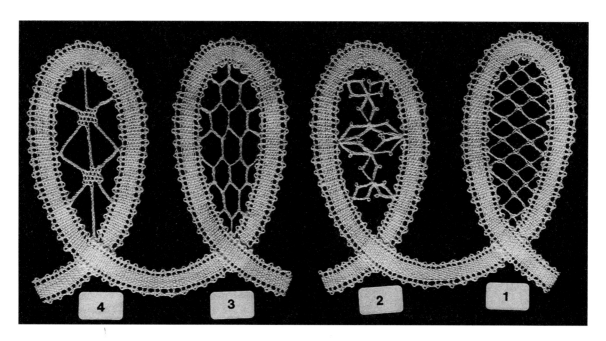

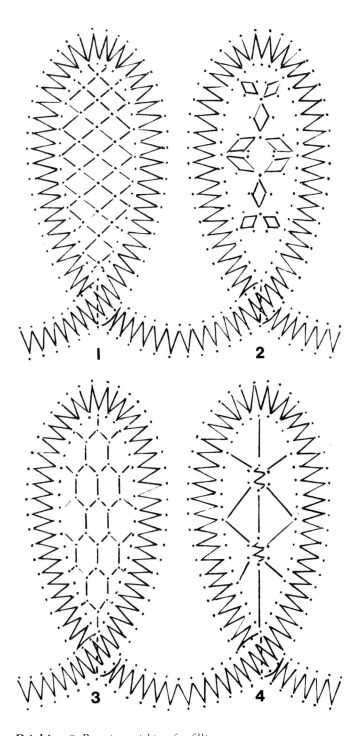

Pricking 8 *Practice pricking for filling spaces*

Plait and picot filling

The method for working this is similar to that of the filling for Flower 2. It is worked with the worker pair and the outside passive pair from the last point of contact at the edge. The line of work is shown on *diagram 24(i)*.

Larger spaces are filled in the same way but it sometimes takes a little time to discover the path you need to follow in order to make the entire filling in one piece, ending at the commencing pin. Two examples of this are seen in *diagram 24 ((ii) and (iii))*.

Hexagonal filling

This filling is worked with two pairs of bobbins but the threads are not taken out from the work in progress as they do not return to the starting point. Thus two pairs are sewn in at a suitable place at the edge. The method of working uses the zigzag line (*diagram 25(ii)*) as a plait. The vertical lines formed by working false plaits use one of the pairs from the main plait. However, there are places where this is not possible, especially at the edges.

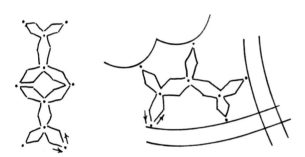

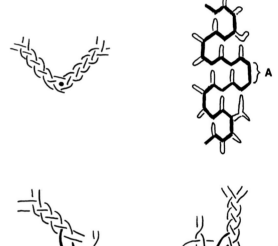

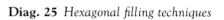

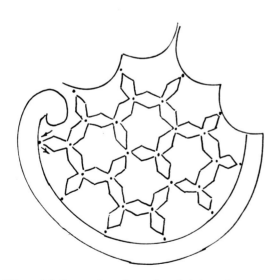

Diag. 24 *Suggestions for paths of plait and picot fillings*

Diag. 25 *Hexagonal filling techniques*

At the points of the zigzag plait where a sewing will be made at the next row of work, put in a pin and twist one pair so that the sewing is made more easily (*diagram 25(i)*). It is sometimes necessary to run the plait over the top of an edge twisted passive pair. This is shown as area A on *diagram 25(ii)*. In this instance, the plait is sewn in as per *diagram 25(iii)* and sewn out as *diagram 25(iv)* shows.

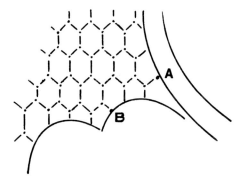

Diag. 26
False plait techniques for hexagonal fillings

Because the outline of the filling is irregular, it may be necessary to sew in and finish a plait at the end of one zigzag line and to start a new one at a different place for the next line, as shown in *diagram 26(i)*.

To make a false plait from a plait, work to the place where it starts and put in a support pin as in *diagram 26(ii)*. Now work the false plait and continue the main plait, starting with a whole stitch to ensure that the unused pair is not twisted. Make sure that the plait is worked tightly and that a hole is not left where the threads have departed and then rejoined the main plait.

'Snowflake' filling

In this filling three plaits are formed and meet in an area of half stitch before separating. To work it, six pairs of bobbins are required for each snowflake and two pairs are sewn into the edge at each starting point.

Make the three plaits and start the half-stitch block by putting in a pin at the top between the two pairs of the middle plait. The right-hand pair becomes the worker. Follow *diagram 27(i)* which shows the route of the worker. Every stitch is a half stitch and both pairs of each plait are worked through when they are added in and taken out again.

The bottom pin is enclosed by the whole stitch which starts the middle plait.

Complete the middle plait and then work the side plaits, either sewing to the edge or carrying on with the next snowflake as the pattern indicates.

A variation for the plaits is to work picots half way between each snowflake. If the snowflake is slightly larger two extra rows are sometimes worked in the middle of the half stitch block.

Diagram 27(ii) shows a larger area of the filling.

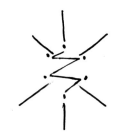

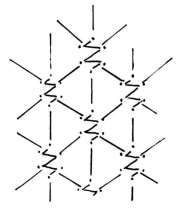

Diag. 27
'Snowflake' filling

33

Plait and picot edge

When making a mat in Bruges Flower lace the pattern often indicates a decorative plait and picot edge. This is to unite parts of the design which would otherwise form an untidy and weak overall shape.

Diagram 28(i) shows two of the different forms this edge may take. The border is worked after all the rest of the outer edge is finished and is joined to that with simple sewings. It is best to work double picots rather than single knotted ones and to use a thick pin to form them. Where two plaits cross, work a 'windmill' or 4-pair crossing as shown in diagram 28(ii). Each pair of bobbins is used as if it were a single thread and a whole stitch is worked, putting the pin in the centre. Re-start each plait after the crossing by working a whole stitch.

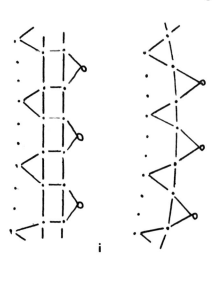

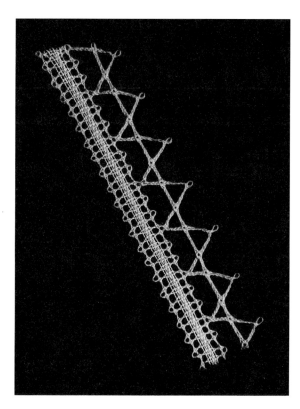

Plait and picot edge

Diag. 28 Plait and picot edge

6
Helpful hints on techniques

Thread lengths

The amount of thread to use on bobbins is sometimes difficult to assess, so helpful suggestions are included under the headings that follow. The lengths of thread given are the amounts required to work the lace. About 50 cm (20 in) must be added to the total length given to keep it from slipping off the bobbin.

There will often be thread left over on the bobbins. This is unavoidable but it is better to wind too much thread rather than too little, which would require untidy joins of thread in the work.

Many parts e.g. leaves and fillings require shorter lengths of thread and the leftovers are frequently long enough to be used as passives. A general rule is that if there is enough thread to wind twelve times round the bobbin, there is sufficient thread. Another tip is to wind one bobbin of a pair very full and to wind off enough from this to the other bobbin for each piece of lace to be worked.

Flowers

When working flowers, check their position in the whole design to decide whether to make the top petal whole stitch or half stitch. Remember that whole stitch produces a heavier effect than half stitch.

Small flowers up to about 16 mm ($\frac{2}{3}$ in) at the widest part of a petal require 50 cm (20 in)

for each outside passive pair worked in whole stitch and twist. The other pairs will each require approximately 150 cm (60 in).

Large flowers The outside passive pairs require 75 cm (29 in) each while other pairs need 300 cm (117 in) on each. Oval and eight-petalled flowers will use at least one third more thread.

Leaves

When working a leaf with a raised centre vein, one side is often shown wider than the other on the pricking. It is better to work up the narrow side in whole stitch as the straight edge lies to the other side of the pin holes. This ensures that the finished effect is of two sides of equal width.

The passives on smaller leaves can be worked with the remnant threads from other parts but make sure the workers are well-filled.

Braids

Braids which go between a flower or a leaf and end in a scroll are best finished with the scroll, and started by hanging the threads in at the flower or leaf.

If working a plait or picot filling make sure the passive pair that is used for this has enough thread on it.

If a braid is long it is best to fill the workers as they will frequently be used for a plaited filling as well. The centre passive threads require double the length of the braid on each bobbin, but the whole stitch and twist edge passives will require more. Make sure that there is enough on the edge passives, which will be used for an integral filling with the workers.

Joinings and fillings

A join is always worked at the last point possible because the loop needed to sew into is already there. The exact number of pairs required for different fillings is not stated on any of the patterns although it is not complicated to assess this. On many occasions it is possible to sew in pairs into the side lace and then continue with them in the filling e.g. in Torchon ground and plait and picot fillings.

Plaited fillings are of course catered for during the main work. Hexagonal fillings may need plenty of thread in large areas. Torchon ground can be made with remnant threads.

Pivot pins

Always let the worker pair build up the pin and remain close to it. The work will give

the impression of a tent with the pivot pin as the central pole. When the pin is taken out, the threads all lie flat and tidily.

The patterns

All the lace shown in this book has been worked in BOUC 50 Fil de Lin or DMC Cordonnet 60 unless specifically stated.

Although the number of passives we used is quoted, if a different make or type of thread is used it is essential to work a sample first to ensure a correct finish.

Work each design in the order stated on each instruction e.g. for Motif 1, work the flower first, braid next, then the leaves and the filling last.

Detailed techniques for each design can be found at the beginning of the book in the relevant section. Within each section, the patterns have been put as far as possible in progressing order of difficulty.

It should be possible to make all the patterns after working the practice pieces. Where two worker pairs are required this indicates a straight edge will be worked for a raised vein.

7
Motifs

These motifs will help the student of Bruges Flower lace to put into practice the basic techniques described in previous sections, before attempting some of the larger, more complex designs.

Motif 1

Flower 2 6 passives + 1 worker pair.
Braid 5 passives + 1 worker pair.
Leaf 1 11 passives + 1 worker pair.

The flower centre is worked using the plait and picot filling. The other filled area is worked in Torchon ground with two twists between the pins.

Motif No 1

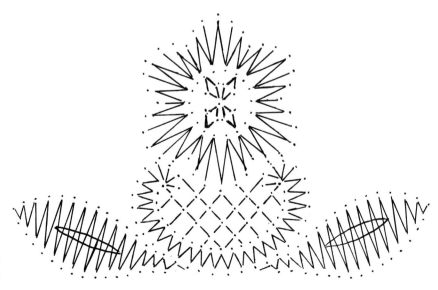

Pricking 9
Motif No 1

Motif 2

Flower 2   6 passives + 1 worker.
Braid   5 passives + 1 worker.
Leaf 4   5 passives + 2 workers.

The braid in this design is the practice one (No 4), involving crossing braids with scrolls at each end.

Motif No 2

Pricking 10 *Motif No 2*

Motif 3

Flower 1   9 passives + 1 worker.
Braid and triple leaf   5 passives + 1 worker adding two more pairs for the leaves.

Start the braid by working the scroll and, at the beginning of the first leaf, add in the two extra pairs so that there are six passives and two workers. The central vein is a straight edge as in Leaf 5. Work the plait and picot filling at the same time as the braid, commencing at the last pin hole that is common to both.

Pricking 11 *Motif No 3*

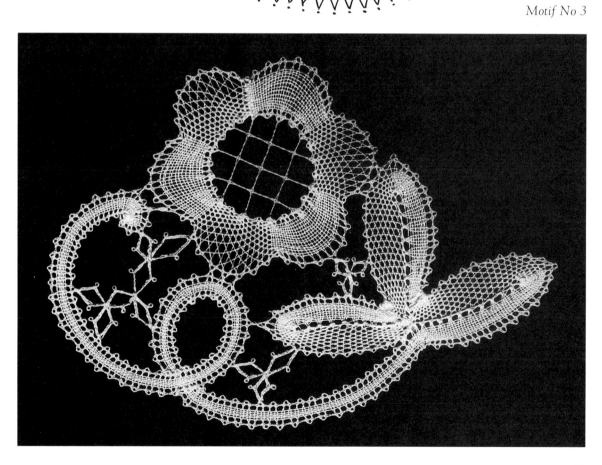

Motif No 3

Motif 4

Flower 2   9 passives + 1 worker.
Leaf 4   6 passives + 2 workers.
Braid   9 passives + 1 worker.

The double leaf with raised central vein is
started at the centre base with four passives
and two workers. The extra two passives
are added on the third and fifth rows of
working. These two pairs will be taken out
at the same position before finishing and
sewing in the threads.

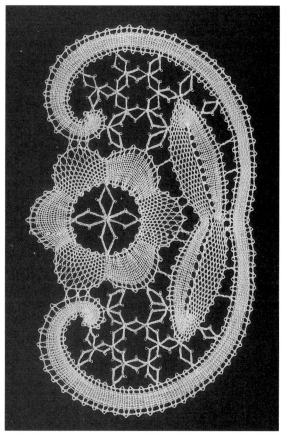

Motif No 4

Pricking 12
Motif No 4

Motif 5

Flower 2   9 passives + 1 worker.
Braid with scrolls   6 passives + 1 worker.
Inner braid   6 passives + 1 worker.

After the flower has been made, work the
braids with scrolls by commencing each at
the flower. Then the inner braid can be
worked, ensuring that the plait and picot
filling is made at the same time.

Motif No 5

Pricking 13 *Motif No 5*

Motif 6

Flower 1 8 passives + 1 worker.
Braid and triple leaf 5 5 passives + 1 worker adding an extra pair for the leaf.
Leaf with open vein 1 7 passives + 1 worker.
Braid with scrolls 6 passives + 1 worker.

At the beginning of the triple leaf one extra pair is added to work a straight edge vein. This pair is discarded just before the end of the third section.

The side leaves are worked as Leaf No 1, twisting the worker to make the open central vein. Make sure that pairs are taken out before the tip to ensure a tidy, pointed end.

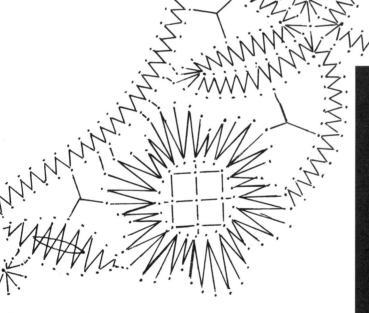

Pricking 14 *Motif No 6*

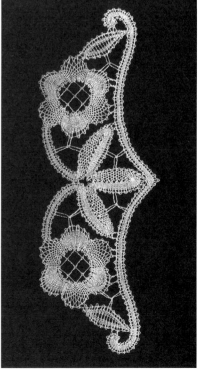

Motif No 6

42

Motif No 7

Motif 7

Flower 5 passives + 1 worker.
Braids 5 passives + 1 worker.

The small filling in the centre of the flower is made with the worker pair only, by making false plaits and joining them at the centre with a sewing when working the final false plait. The central filling is the Snowflake filling.

Pricking 15 *Motif No 7*

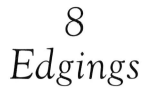

8
Edgings

By combining the various elements of a design in a slightly different manner they can be put to a wide range of uses and made into a number of shapes. We have tried to show this adaptability within each pattern.

The first edgings are narrow and simple, but those towards the end of this section become wider and more complex in their techniques and construction.

Sampler edging

Flower 9 passives + 1 worker.
Inner braid 7 passives + 1 worker.
Outer braid 9 passives + 1 worker.

This design provides the opportunity to practise the various fillings in Bruges Flower lace and to work two of the less familiar braids. The wide outer braid has eyelets whilst the inner, petal-shaped one has alternate whole and half stitch areas separated by short plaits.

left side

Pricking 16(a)
sampler edging – left side

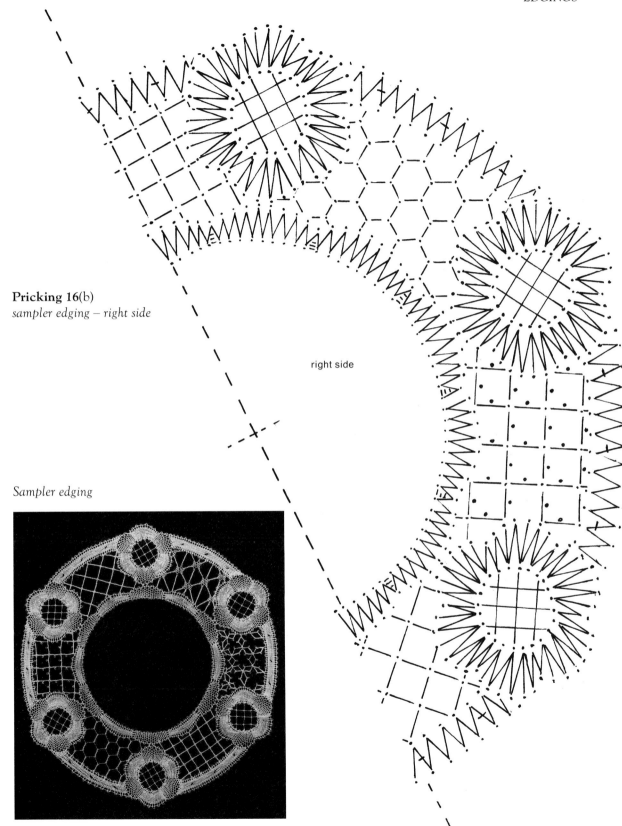

Pricking 16(b)
sampler edging – right side

right side

Sampler edging

Pricking 17
Edge No 1 – waves

Edge No 1 (waves)

Main braid   6 passives + 1 worker.
Little braid   5 passives + 1 worker.
Leaf   5 passives + 1 worker.
Add in five more pairs of passives and
another worker to the main braid as it
widens to separate – see the technique for
dividing braids (p. 16). Make sure that there
is enough thread on the worker for the
continuous braid. If this pair is kept to the
right when working, the same bobbins
(except one) will run the length of the work.
The right-hand bobbin of the first new pair
must also be fully wound.

Keep the other new pairs to the left side as
far as possible, as they are intended for the
braid with the scroll. Thus the four whole
stitch pairs to the right are retained in the
continuous braid.

The filling is worked as plaits with
'windmill' crossings: the dotted lines show
the pattern repeat.

Use this to decorate a skirt hem.

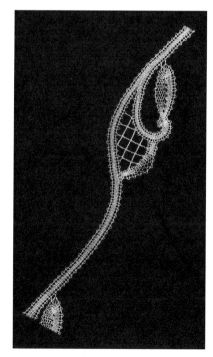

*Edge No 1
(waves)*

Edge No 2
(flowers and scrolled braids)

Flower 6 passives + 1 worker.
Braid 5 passives + 1 worker.

The plait and picot filling in the centre of
the flower can be replaced with false plaits
joined at the centre, if desired.

This design can be used with or without the
corner braid. It looks lovely appliquéd
down the front of a blouse or mounted
round the edge of a lampshade.

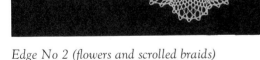

Edge No 2 (flowers and scrolled braids)

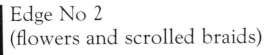

Pricking 18 *Edge No 2 –
flowers and scrolled braids*

47

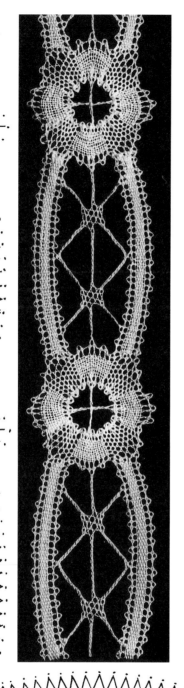

Edge No 3
(flowers and snowflakes)

Flower   6 passives + 1 worker.
Braid   5 passives + 1 worker.

The flower centre is made by working two false plaits and joining them in the middle with a sewing. This is a very versatile design and can be used for square, rectangular or hexagonal edgings. The diagram shows the positioning of the elements for the hexagonal version.

Although the worked sample has no corner, the pricking shows the arrangement for a square or rectangular edge.

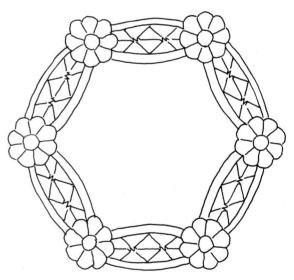

Diag. 29 *Alternative arrangement of elements for Edge No 3 – flowers and snowflakes*

Pricking 19
Edge No 3 – flowers and snowflakes

48

Edge No 4 (oval)

Flower braid   6 passives + 2 workers.
Flower petals   9 passives + 1 worker.
Main braid   7 passives + 1 worker.
Double leaf   6 passives + 2 workers.
Little braid   6 passives + 1 worker.

A feature of this design is the oval, ten-petalled flower at each end of the shape, whilst the centre of each side features double leaves.

The main braid unites these two parts into the overall oval shape. The pricking has been printed in sections to fit the page size but the diagram shows their assembly.

Two copies of the pricking are required to make the whole shape, which is depicted mounted on a pillow case.

Edge No 4 (oval design on pillowcase)

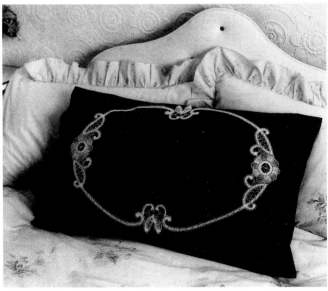

Diag. 30
Assembly of pricking for Oval Edge No 4

Pricking 20(a)

Edge No 4 – end of oval shape

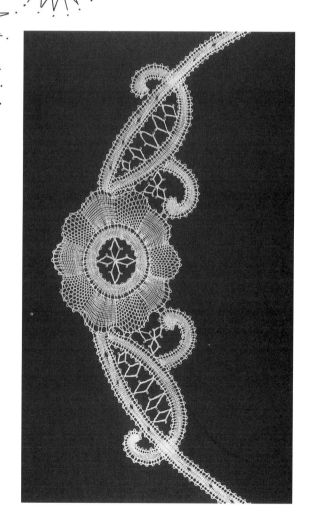

Detail of the end section of Edge No 4 (oval)

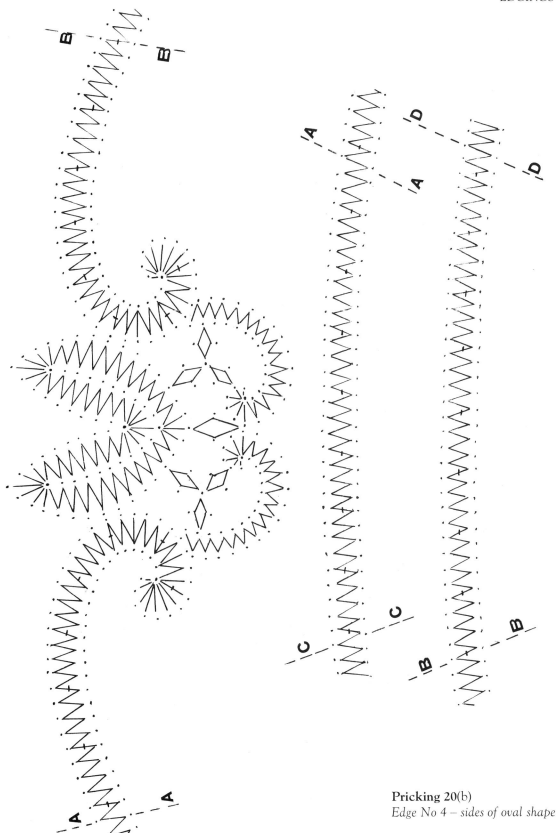

Pricking 20(b)
Edge No 4 – sides of oval shape

Edge No 5 (round)

Flower braid 4 passives + 2 workers.
Flower petals 5 passives + 1 worker.
Braid 7 passives + 1 worker.
Leaf 7 passives + 2 workers.

This pretty circular edging is shown mounted on a pillow case. The braid can be worked in whole stitch with eyelets or, alternatively, in half stitch for contrast. If it is worked in half stitch, two fewer pairs of passives are required.

The complete circle consists of three pattern repeats as shown in the diagram. The size of the design, once again, means that the sections will need careful joining before the lace can be worked.

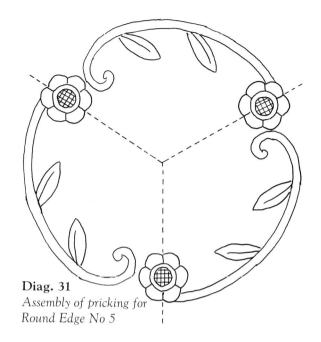

Diag. 31
Assembly of pricking for Round Edge No 5

Edge No 5 (round edge on pillowcase)

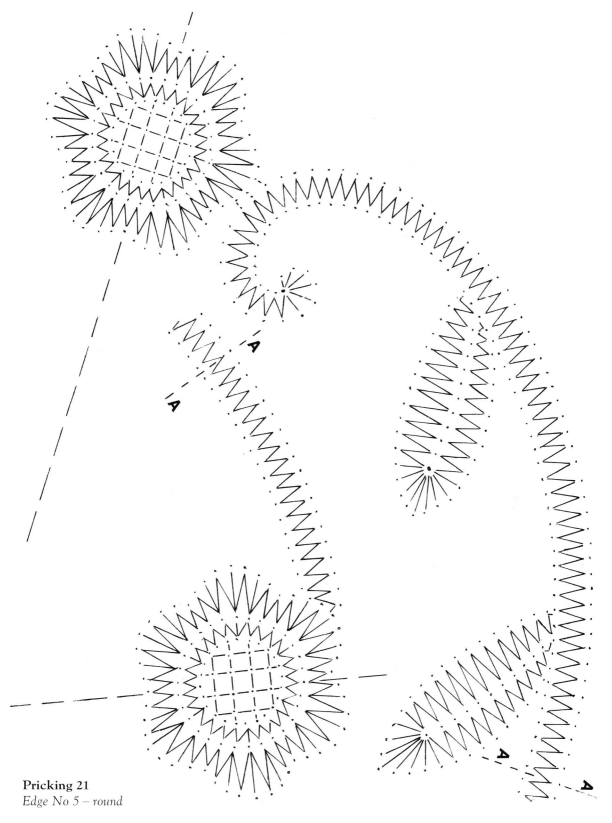

Pricking 21
Edge No 5 – round

Edge No 6 (round hexagon)

Flower braid   5 passives + 1 worker.
Flower petals   10 passives + 1 worker.
Main braid   6 passives + 1 worker.

The main filling in this design is the hexagonal one, to echo the hexagonal centre shape. The other filling is the plait and picot filling.

The pricking is $\frac{1}{6}$ of the whole shape.

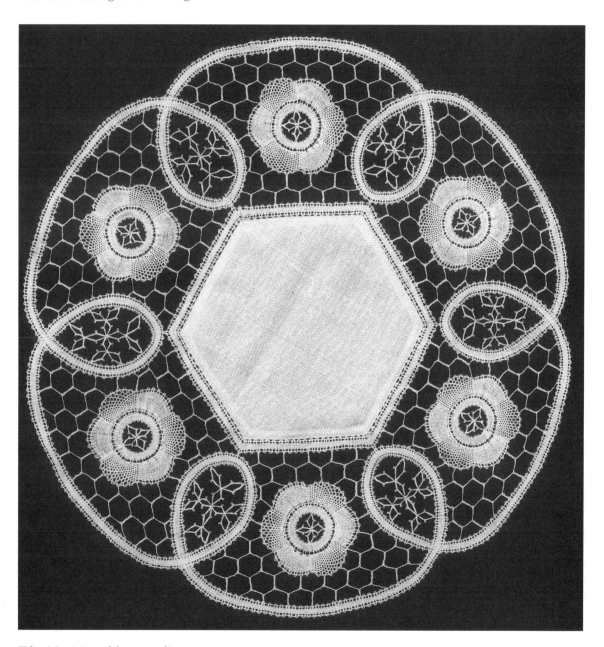

Edge No 6 (round/hexagonal)

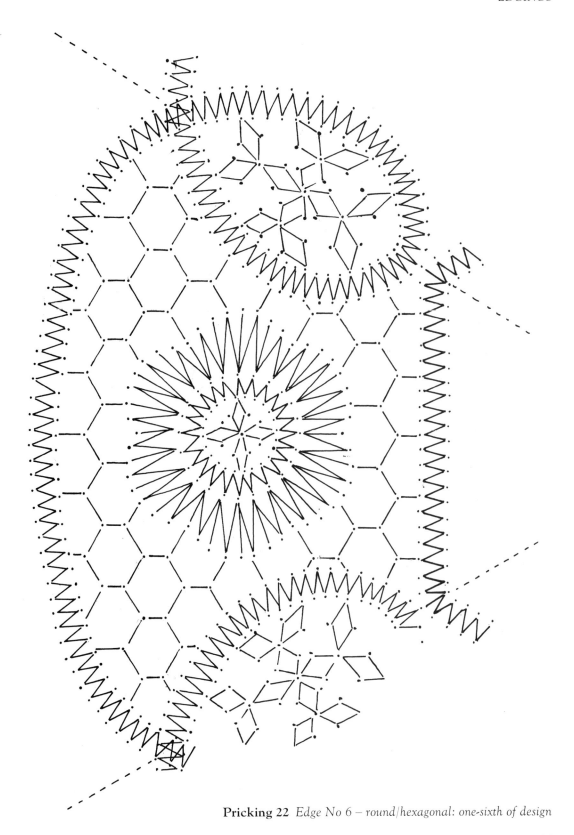

Pricking 22 *Edge No 6 – round/hexagonal: one-sixth of design*

Edge No 7 (without corners)

Flower 9 passives + 1 worker.
Braid 5 passives + 1 worker.
Leaf 4 passives + 1 worker.
Pricking 23a shows a continuous straight edging without corners. Note that as the half stitch area of the leaf narrows towards the base, some pairs must be discarded before the leaf threads are sewn into the braid.

Pricking 23b shows that by reversing the braid and leaf area, it is mirrored on either side of the flower. In this way a single motif can be made instead of a continuous one.

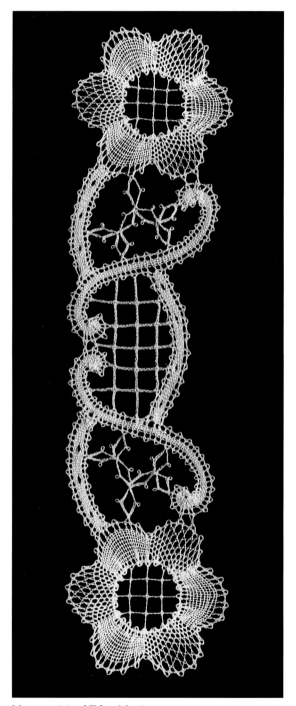

A single motif from Edge No 7

Version (ii) of Edge No 8

Pricking 23(a)
Continuous Edge No 7

Pricking 23(b)
Single motif from continuous edge elements

Edge No 8
(cornerless floral design)

Flower   6 passives + 1 worker.
Braid   5 passives + 1 worker.

In *diagram 32(i)* the scrolled braids are worked after the flowers, and the small braids last. The plait and picot filling is worked at the same time as the small braids.

Diagram 32(ii) depicts an alternative design made by substituting the upper flower with an eyelet braid and plaited filling. The eyelet braid requires seven passives and a worker.

Diagram 32(iii) shows that by working only a single flower with scrolled braids on either side, a pretty single motif is produced.

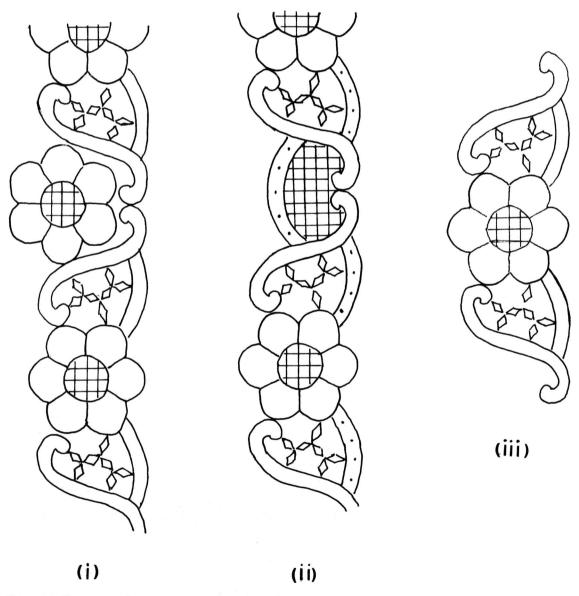

(i)　　　　**(ii)**

(iii)

Diag. 32 *Suggestions for arrangement of motifs – Edge No 8*

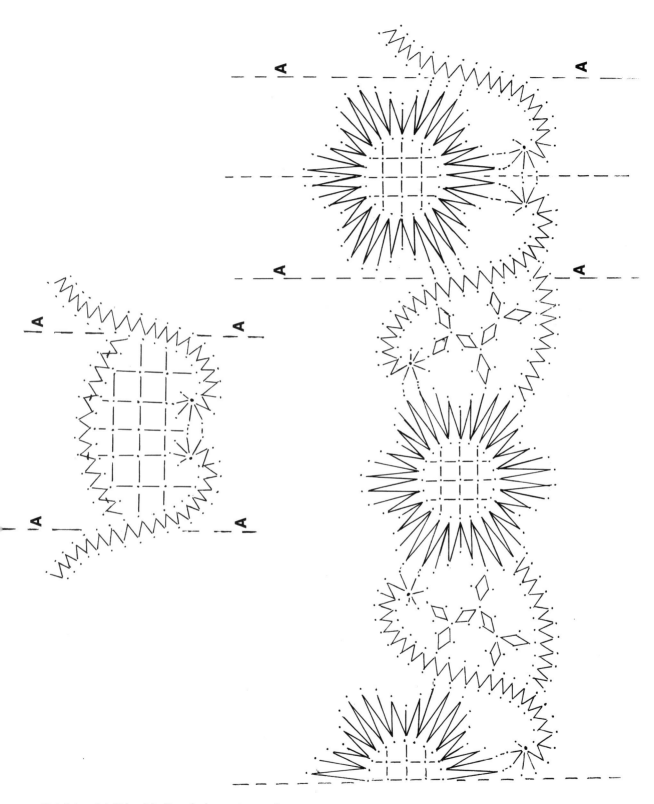

Pricking 24 *Edge No 8 and alternative section*

9
Crosses

Bruges is a city steeped in religious history that dates from the time of the Crusades. It seems appropriate that its own special lace lends itself to the design of the Christian cross with such beautiful results. The patterns in this section depict a very small selection of the many possible permutations.

Cross No 1

Cross No 2

Cross No 4

Cross No 3

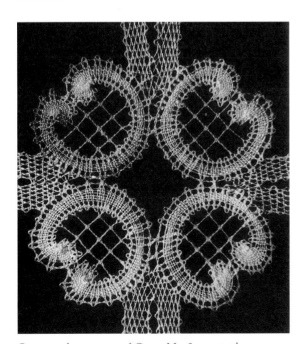

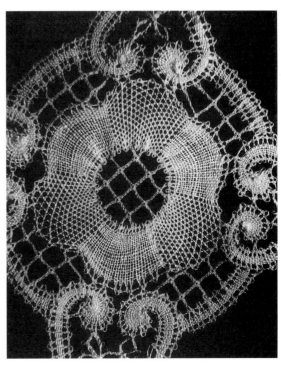

Centre enlargement of Cross No 3 – note the fluffiness of linen thread

Centre enlargement of Cross No 4

Cross No 1

Flower braid   3 passives + 1 worker.
Flower petals   7 passives + 1 worker.
Main braid   7 passives + 1 worker.

This is a very simple, clean shape and is suitable for a relative beginner to this type of lace.

Pricking 25 *Cross No 1*

Cross No 2

Flower braid   3 passives + 1 worker.
Flower petals   6 passives + 1 worker.
Braid   6 passives + 1 worker.

This design is different, as it is a 'standing' cross. The bottom arm has been shaped to give the impression of a wrought-iron base.

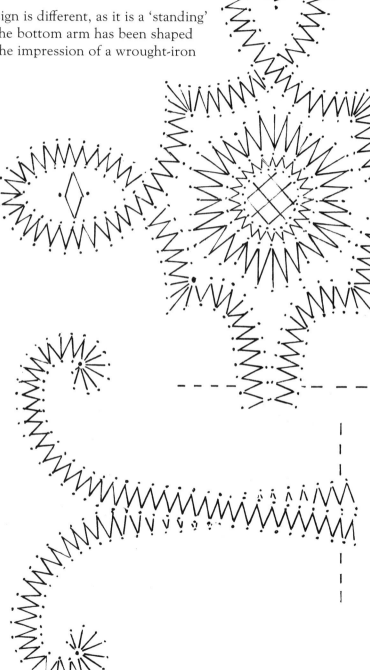

Pricking 26 *Cross No 2*

Cross No 3

Scrolled braid 5 passives + 1 worker.
Half-stitch braid 6 passives + 1 worker.

This design is worked in BOUC 80 Fil de
Lin. Although a simple shape, it is unusual
in that there is no flower in the design and
the main arms are worked in half stitch
with whole stitch and twist for the edge
passives. This, combined with the use of a
thinner thread, produces a delicate effect
and makes the central whole stitch scrolled
braids more prominent.

Pricking 27 *Cross No 3*

Cross No 4

Flower   13 passives + 1 worker.
Braid   5 passives + 1 worker.
Once again the thread used in BOUC 80 Fil

de Lin. It is a more elaborate version of the first cross. Each arm is worked as a separate braid with scrolled ends. The ring of braid round the flower produces the effect of a Celtic cross.

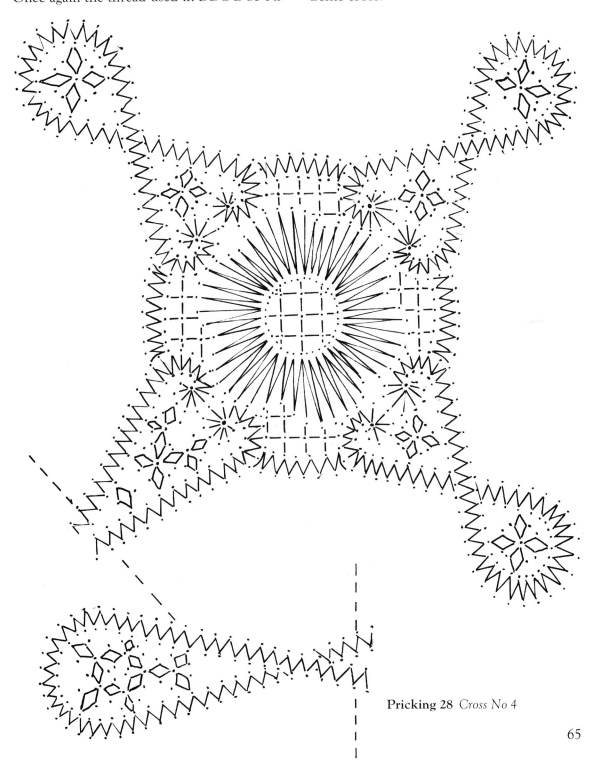

Pricking 28 *Cross No 4*

10
Collars and cuffs

The addition of a lace collar to a dress or blouse can be tricky, as every garment has a differently-shaped neckline. It is preferable, if possible, to make the collar first and then make the garment to fit the lace. If this is not possible, double-check the shape and adapt the pricking before working if necessary. This saves many hours of work that might produce less-than-satisfactory results.

Peter Pan collar

Edge braid   6 passives + 1 worker.
Front flower   8 passives + 1 worker.
Centre flower   7 passives + 1 worker.
Rear flower   6 passives + 1 worker.
Braid between flowers   4 passives + 1 worker.
Leaf with braid   8 passives + 1 worker.
Small leaf   6 passives + 1 worker.

This is a versatile collar with alternative shapes at the back and front.

Begin the leaves at the centre flower and lose four pairs of passives at the start of the braid.

The edge can be worked completely in whole stitch if preferred, although the collar in the photograph has alternate whole and half stitch sections. The front and back end alternate shapes have been given. The lines for matching up the prickings are clearly marked.

Peter Pan collar showing the rounded ends version and the oval flower earrings

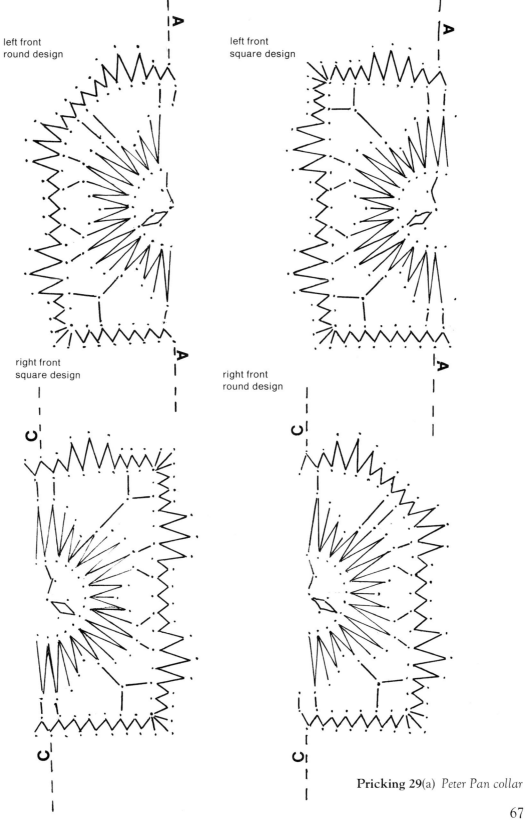

left front
round design

left front
square design

right front
square design

right front
round design

Pricking 29(a) *Peter Pan collar*

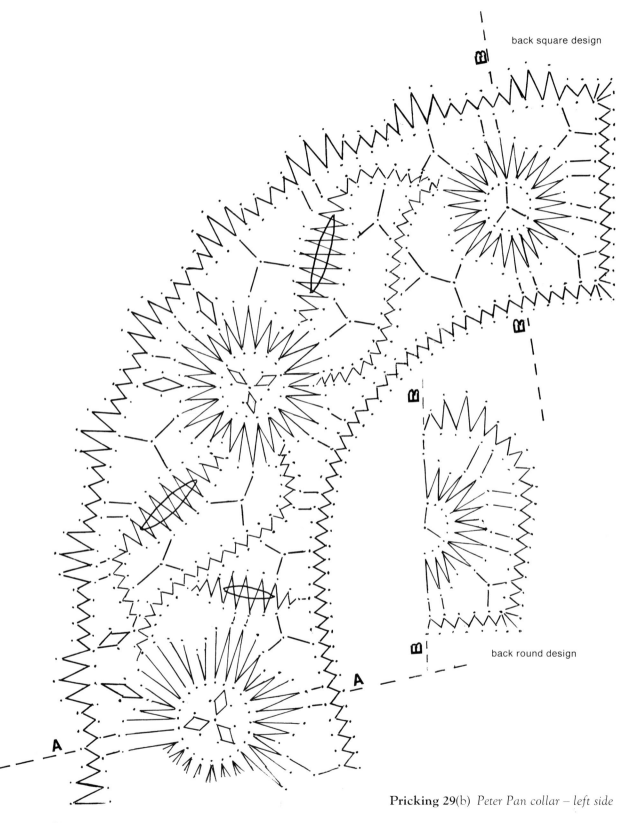

back square design

back round design

Pricking 29(b) *Peter Pan collar – left side*

back square design

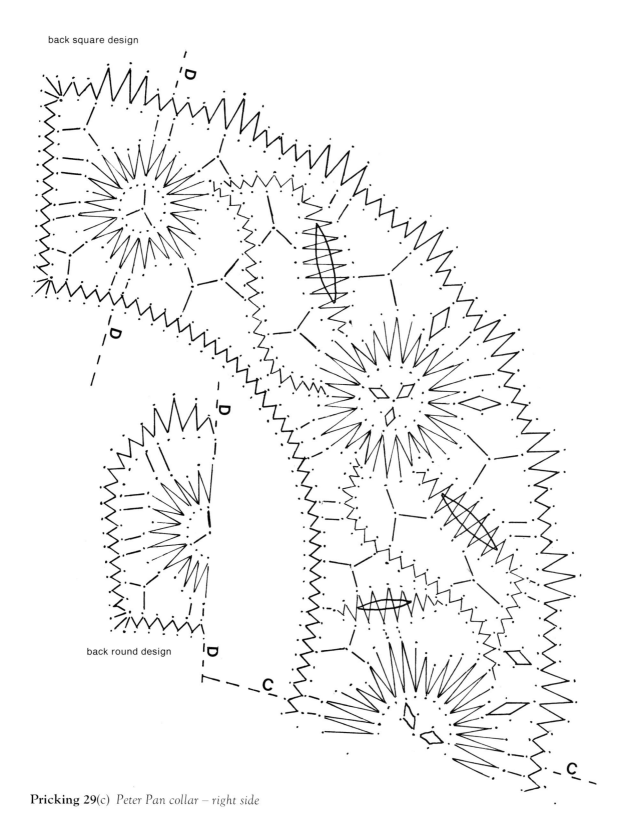

back round design

Pricking 29(c) *Peter Pan collar – right side*

Collar and cuff set

Braid   5 passives + 1 worker.

An extra pair must be added at the start of each leaf and discarded on its completion.

This pattern is unusual for Bruges Flower lace in that it is made all-in-one, without joining separate sections with sewings. The simple cuff complements the collar, which can be worked in two halves as shown in the pricking. The collar in the photograph was worked as a single unit using the small piece of pricking at the centre back to unite the other two sections.

We have omitted any filling in the large loops of braid but, if desired, one can be worked in these areas.

Collar from the collar and cuff set with pearl drop earrings

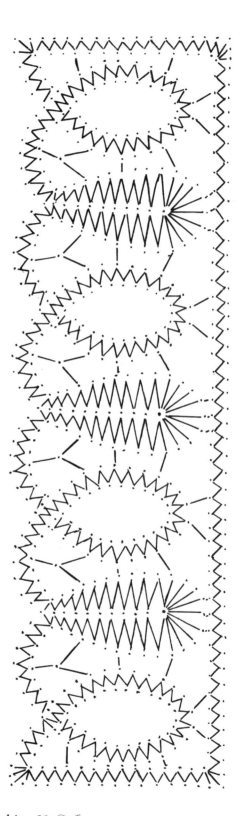

Pricking 30 *Cuff*

70

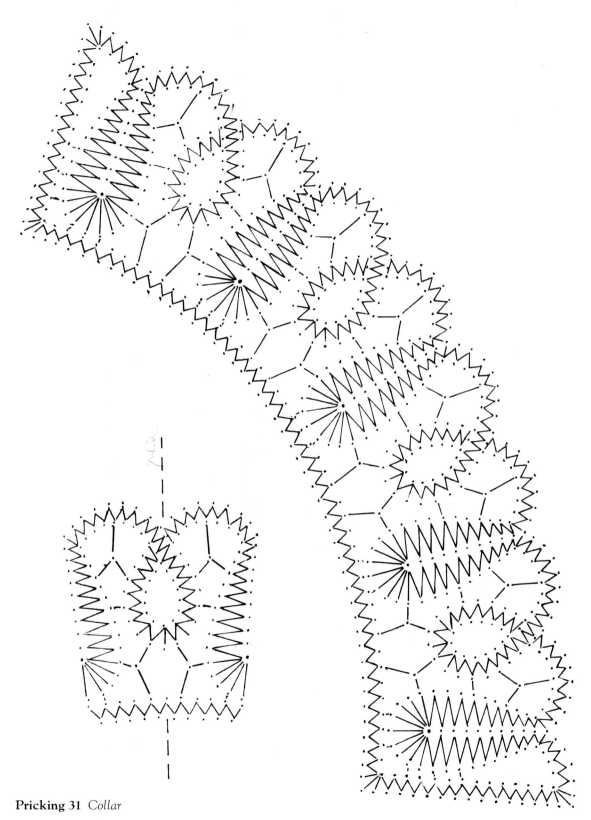

Pricking 31 *Collar*

Cuff No 2 (flowers and scrolls)

Flower   9 passives + 1 worker.
Braid   6 passives + 1 worker.

This cuff pattern and the following one are intended to be decorative designs for sleeve cuffs which could also be used as continuous shapes to adorn skirts or as insertions on blouses.

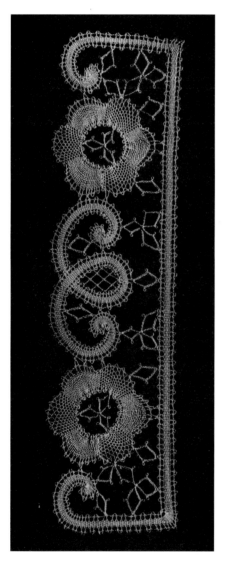

Cuff No 2 (flowers and scrolls)

Cuff No 3 (leaves and flower)

Flower   9 passives + 1 worker.
Braid   6 passives + 1 worker.
Braid and leaves   6 passives + 1 worker.

An extra pair must be added to the braid to work the leaves which have been made without raised centre veins.

These designs also look very attractive if appliquéd to the ends of table mats, for instance.

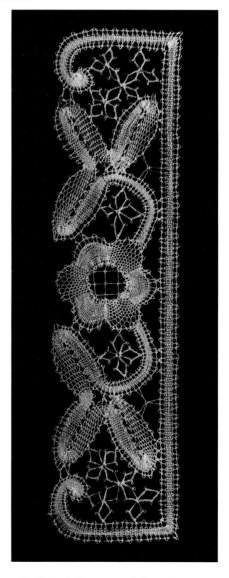

Cuff No 3 (leaves and flowers)

Pricking 32 *Cuff No 2 – flowers and scrolls*

Pricking 33 *Cuff No 3 – leaves and flowers*

Design for a v-shaped neckline

Flower   9 passives + 1 worker.
Double leaf   6 passives + 2 workers.
Braids   5 passives + 1 worker.

The left side of the pricking is a mirror image of the right side. This edge design is intended to decorate a v-shaped neck of a garment. It could also be used as a corner motif by opening up the double leaf and making the two halves at right angles to each other.

As shown in *diagram 33*, by using the flower and positioning the scrolled braids on either side of it, a single motif is formed. This could echo the main design and decorate the hem of the same garment, or it could be used as a feature on a pocket, for example.

Note   Although this pattern is neither a collar nor a cuff, it has been included in this section of patterns as it was originally conceived to decorate a collar.

Diag. 33 *Alternative shapes for V-shaped neck edging*

Design for V-shaped neckline with the round flower earrings

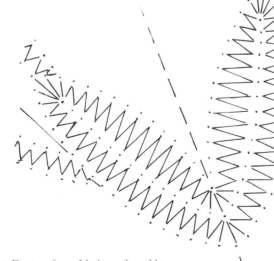

Pricking 34 *Design for a V-shaped neckline*

11
All-lace mats

Bruges Flower lace lends itself very well to the design of mats with no other fabric than the lace itself.

In this section we have included designs for a variety of sizes, from a small doyley to large mats which have necessitated dividing their prickings into sections. There are instructions on the methods for assembling these prickings.

Several of the large mats also have extra sections which can enlarge them further. Once again we have tried to make the most of the versatility of these designs.

Mat No 1 (small round doyley)

Flower   9 passives + 1 worker.
Main braid   6 passives + 1 worker.
Middle braid   4 passives + 1 worker.

This is a pretty design which is useful as a drinks mat, perhaps. The inner plait and picot filling is worked at the same time as the centre braid.

Mat No 1

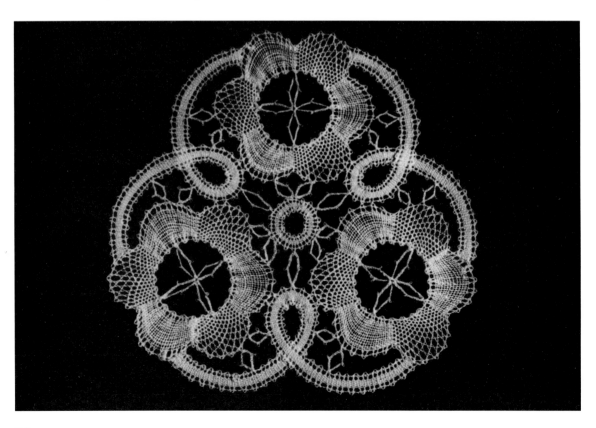

Pricking 35 *Mat No 1 – small round doyley*

Mat No 2 (oval)

Flower braid   6 passives + 2 workers.
Flower petals   9 passives + 1 worker.
Braid   10 passives + 1 worker.
Leaf   5 passives + 1 worker.

The leaves are worked without the second worker in this lace (see photograph), to contrast with the raised vein in the flower. If a completely symmetrical shape is needed, the leaves can be worked in whole stitch from the tip inwards, making the central vein by twisting the workers. This would require a total of nine passives and one worker for each leaf.

The main filling is Torchon ground with three twists between the pins. Only half the pricking is given.

Mat No 2

Pricking 36 *Mat No 2 – oval: one-half of design*

Mat No 3 (large oval)

Oval flower   8 passives + 1 worker.
Flower braid   4 passives + 1 worker.
Triple leaves   5 passives + 2 workers.
Braid   7 passives + 1 worker.
Small leaf and braid   4 passives + 1 worker.

The triple leaf at the side of the flower requires three more passive pairs as the centre section widens. The plait and picot filling at each end can be replaced, if desired, by a continuation of the main hexagonal filling in this area.

The pricking for this mat must be assembled from the quarter sections given and will require two complete copies of each section.

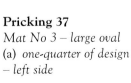

Pricking 37
Mat No 3 – large oval
(a) *one-quarter of design*
– left side

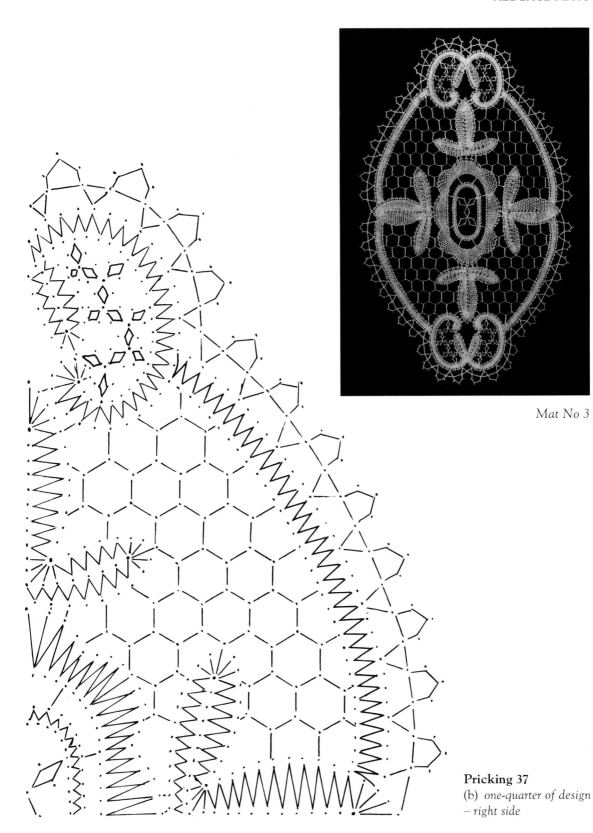

Mat No 3

Pricking 37
(b) *one-quarter of design
– right side*

Mat No 4 (round)

Flower   10 passives + 1 worker.
Scrolled braids   8 passives + 1 worker.
Outer braid   7 passives + 2 workers.
Edge petals   7 passives + 1 worker.

When working the outer braid remember to form a straight edge for the part that is at the outer edge, to form the raised vein. It is not necessary to lose a pair for the loops which do not have a straight edge, but merely to use one of the workers as the outside passive pair. This pair is used as a worker again to make the straight edge after the braids have crossed.

The edge petals are all joined with raised sewings to complete the raised vein.

Mat No 4

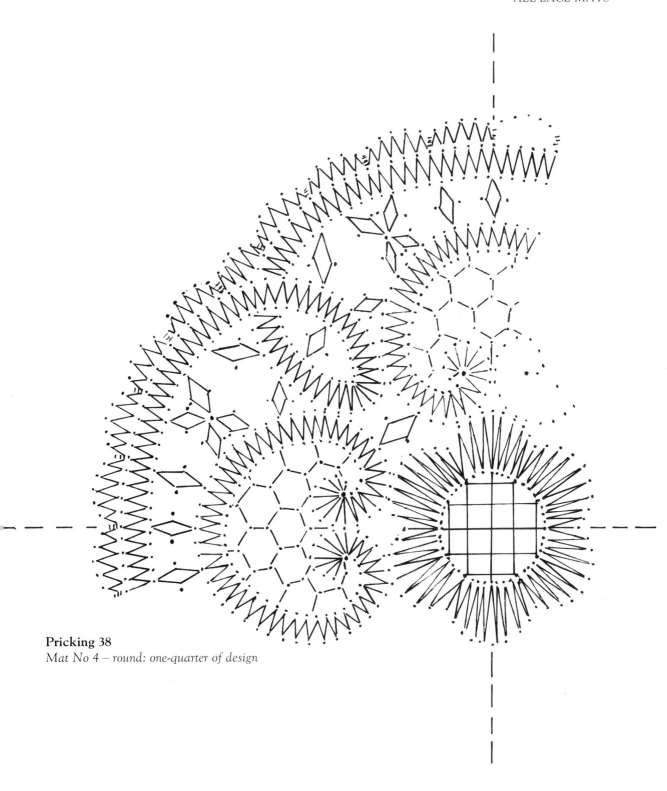

Pricking 38
Mat No 4 – round: one-quarter of design

Mat No 5 (round)

Centre flower braid   7 passives + 2 workers.
Centre flower petals   14 passives + 1 worker.
Petal ring   8 passives + 1 worker.
Braid   7 passives + 1 worker.

Note the use of petals with plaits between each one to make the decorative ring round the flower.

The edge is unusual as the plait and picot area does not go all the way round. It is broken up with the reversed scrolled braids. The ground stitch within these is formed by plaits with 'windmill' crossings. The other grounds are plait and picot ones.

Mat No 5

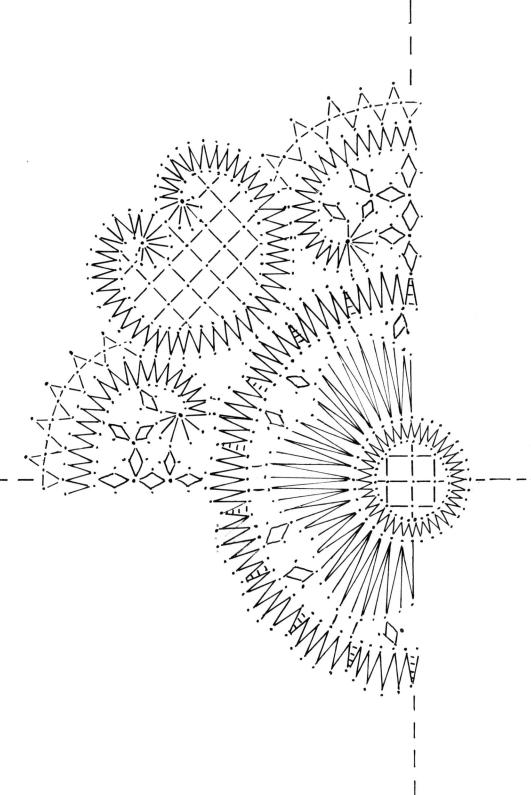

Pricking 39 *Mat No 5 – round: one-quarter of design*

Mat No 6 (large round)

Centre flower   9 passives + 1 worker.
Centre flower braid   4 passives + 1 worker.
Main braid   7 passives + 1 worker.
Edge flower   9 passives + 1 worker.
Outer braid (*with scroll*)   6 passives + 1 worker.

This is the first of three large designs which all have a choice of more than one edge.

The pricking for this design is for one-eighth of the total mat, although the centre flower is complete.

The plaited filling in the loop of the braid has been designed so that the threads can be carried across the braid to work the main 'snowflake' filling. They are sewn in where they join the braid; plaited across the braid; and then sewn out at the appropriate place.

This design can be worked using either of

the two alternative edges, or even left with the outer braid as the edge.

The design of flower and scrolled braids from the outer edge (*pricking 40*) can be used as a single motif.

Pricking 40
Mat No 6 –
large round:
one-eighth
of design

Mat No 6

Diag. 34
*Mat No 6
(large round) –
positions for
alternate
edgings*

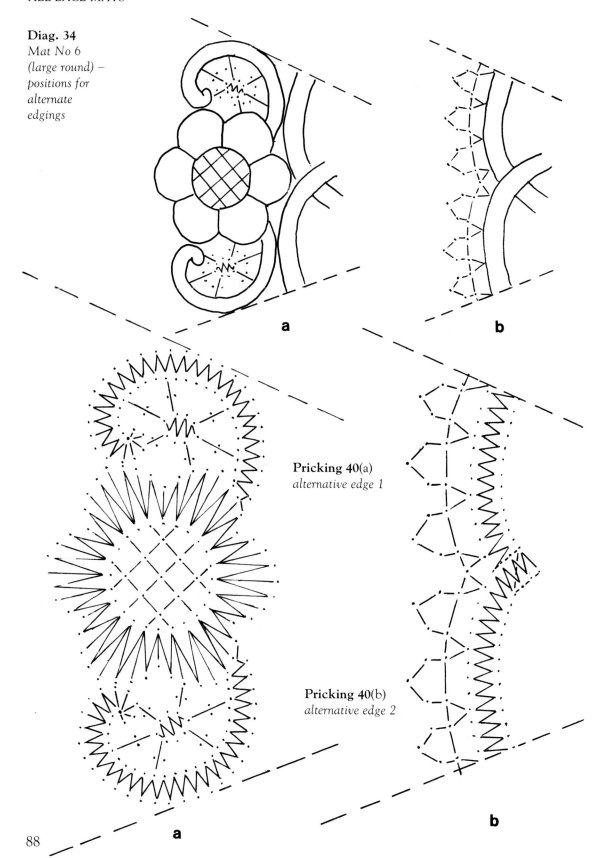

a

b

Pricking 40(a)
alternative edge 1

Pricking 40(b)
alternative edge 2

a

b

Mat No 7 (large oval)

Centre flower braid   6 passives + 2 workers.
Centre flower petals   9 passives + 1 worker.
Triple leaf   7 passives + 2 workers.
Outer braid   7 passives + 1 worker.
Inner braid   5 passives + 1 worker.
Outer oval flower   8 passives + 1 worker.
End leaf   7 passives + 2 workers.

Note   The triple leaf can also be worked as three single leaves. In this case, the centre leaf needs eight passives and two workers and the side leaves seven passives and two workers.

The diagram shows the position of the alternative ends which shorten the design by omitting the end flower and leaf section – *pricking 41(a)*. The gap this leaves in the main pricking is closed with *prickings 41(b) and (c)*.

Mat No 7

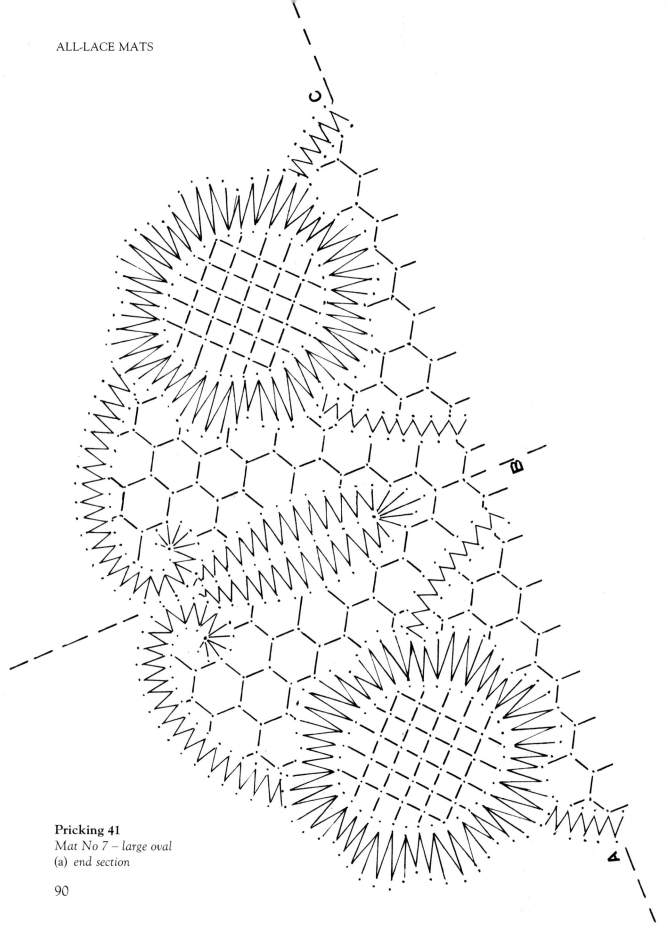

Pricking 41
Mat No 7 – large oval
(a) *end section*

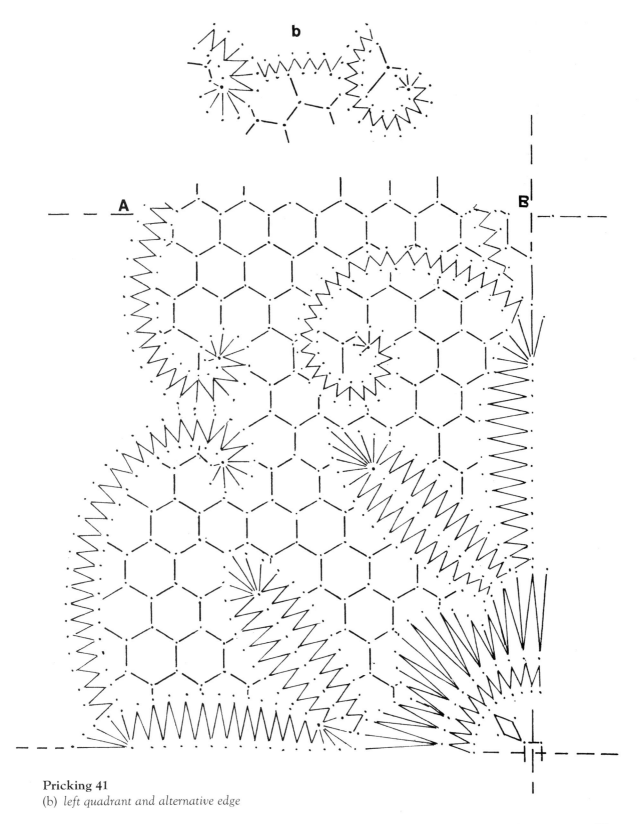

Pricking 41
(b) *left quadrant and alternative edge*

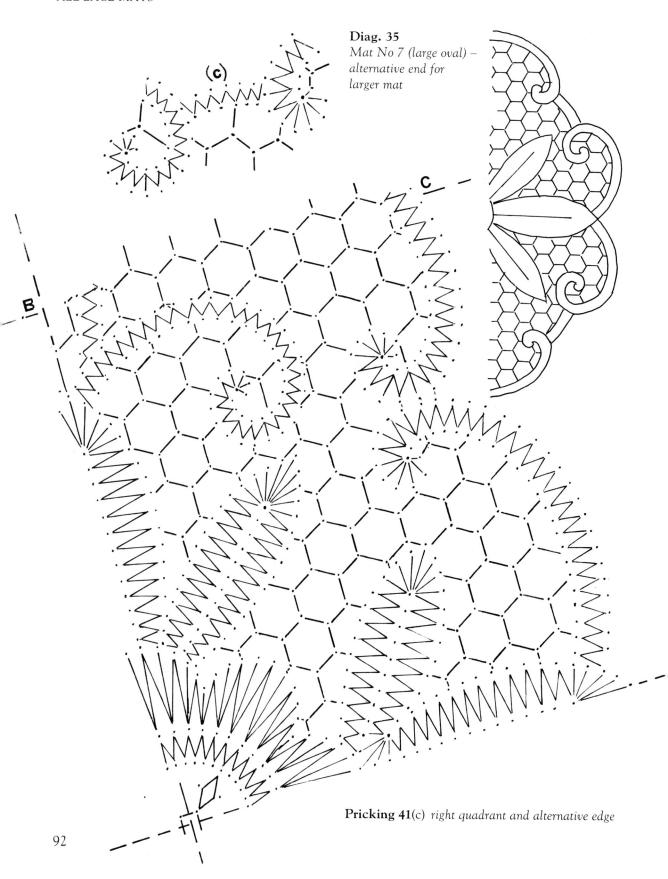

(c)

Diag. 35
Mat No 7 (large oval) –
alternative end for
larger mat

C

B

Pricking 41(c) *right quadrant and alternative edge*

Mat No 8

Large centre flower petals   9 passives + 1 worker.
Large centre flower braid   5 passives + 1 worker.
Braid and scrolls   5 passives + 1 worker.
Other flower   9 passives + 1 worker.

Instead of providing a pricking for the complete mat we have included its individual motifs, and then show some of the ways they can be combined to make the finished pieces of lace.

These suggestions for their arrangement are to make three small mats to complement larger mats with hexagonal fillings:
Diagram 36(i) shows a single flower with two braid motifs.
Diagram 36(ii) has a single flower with four braid motifs.
Diagram 36(iii) uses three flowers and braid motifs laid together to form a triangle.

Mat No 8 with alternative edge

Pricking 42 *Mat No 8 – (large round) pricking of the four main elements*

Diag. 36 *Mat No 8 (large) – suggested motif positions for small mats*

(top left)
Double motif version
of Mat No 8

(top right)
Triple motif version
of Mat No 8

Full version of
Mat No 8

12
For the home

Many people are under the impression that Bruges Flower lace is only used for doyleys and mats. This section of designs will show some other uses around the home. The patterns have all been designed for a specific use but, hopefully, they will inspire designers and lacemakers to produce ideas of their own for the adornment of their homes.

Asymmetric wall hanging

Wall hanging

Large flower   9 passives + 1 worker.
Edge flower   9 passives + 1 worker.
Small flower   8 passives + 1 worker.
Braid   7 passives + 1 worker.
Inside leaf   5 passives + 2 workers.
Right-hand leaf   5 passives + 2 workers.
Larger left leaf   6 passives + 2 workers.

This motif is large and is of asymmetric design. Each flower has a different filling from the others although they can all be made in the same way if you so wish.

Pricking 43 *Asymmetric wall hanging*
(a) *top section*

Pricking 43(b) *bottom section*

Coaster set

Diamond	*Flower*	8 passives + 1 worker.
	Braid	6 passives + 1 worker.
Heart	*Braid*	7 passives + 1 worker.
Club	*Braid*	7 passives + 1 worker.
	Stem	8 passives + 1 worker.
Spade	*Braid*	7 passives + 1 worker.
	Stem	8 passives + 1 worker.

The thread used for these designs is BOUC 100 Fil de Lin. They have been mounted in 90 mm (3½ in) diameter coasters and backed with red or black felt to represent the different coloured suits in a pack of cards.

Coaster set

Pricking 44 *Hearts, spades, diamonds and clubs designs for coasters*

Glass tray

Centre flower   8 passives + 1 worker.
Side flower: Inner braid   4 passives + 2
          workers.
          Petals   6 passives + 1 worker.
Braid   8 passives + 1 worker.

This design is worked in BOUC 80 Fil de Lin. The working lines have been omitted from the flowers to prevent a confusing effect; they are very close together. Half of the pattern is shown in the pricking.

Design in a glass tray

Pricking 45 *Design for glass tray – one-half of pricking*

Study in black and white

Braid   5 passives + 1 worker.
Leaf   6 passives + 1 worker.

One more passive pair must be added to the braid for the half stitch area.

This is Bruges Flower lace at its most versatile. The photograph shows the entirely contrasting effects obtained by using reverse colours. The finished shapes are both square as the designs consist of the same single motif positioned in different ways. Each finished square requires four copies of the pricking.

In the black example the motif is positioned so that the leaf points outwards at each corner, while the other design has the leaves meeting at the centre.

The position of the plait and picot filling is changed for each shape. Although we have worked these ground stitches, we recommend that different ones are used to obtain other effects.

Study in black and white

Diag. 37 *Two versions of motifs for black and white design*

Pricking 46 *Motif used for the black and white design*

Design for a cushion (1)

Flower: Braid   4 passives + 1 worker.
       Petals   10 passives + 1 worker.
Inner braid   6 passives + 1 worker.
Outer braid   7 passives + 1 worker.

The pricking shows $\frac{1}{6}$ of the whole design. If the lace were to be mounted as the edge of a mat with a fabric centre, the stitching and cutting of the material would be intricate but very effective.

Cushion (design No 1)

Pricking 47 *Cushion design No 1 – one-sixth of pricking*

Design for a cushion (2)

Flower   10 passives + 1 worker.
Outer braid   9 passives + 1 worker.
Centre braid   9 passives + 1 worker.

The outer braid, flower and filling are worked in DMC 60 Cordonnet while the centre braid and filling uses DMC 40 Cordonnet which is a thicker thread. The same colour – ecru – is used throughout. This produces a softer effect than white thread, to complement the green cushion. This design can also be used as a mat.

Cushion (design No 2)

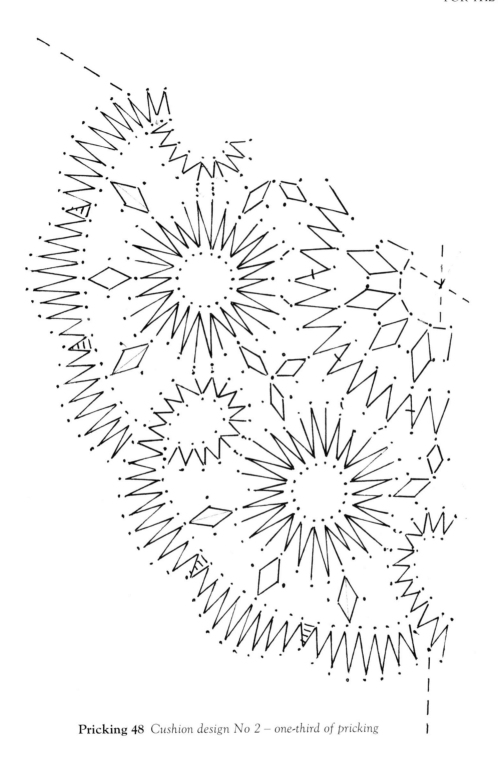

Pricking 48 *Cushion design No 2 – one-third of pricking*

Pricking 49(a)
Basket of flowers – left side

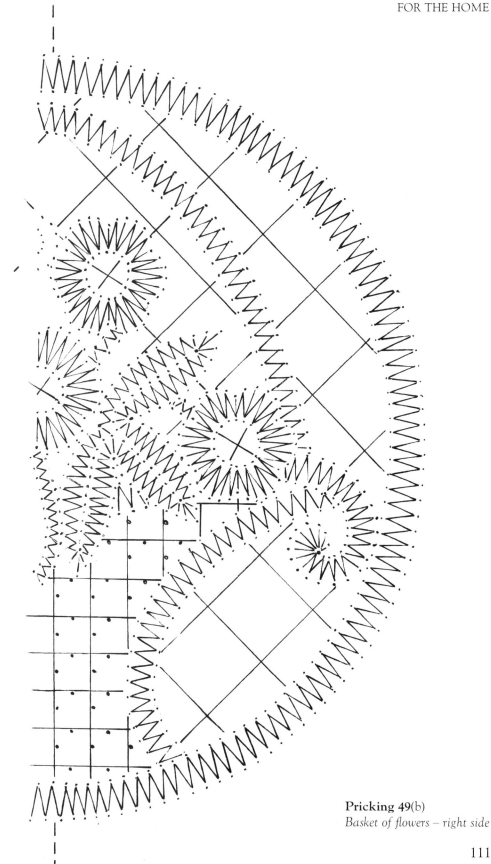

Pricking 49(b)
Basket of flowers – right side

Window decoration (basket of flowers)

Outer ring 8 passives + 1 worker.
Large centre flower 7 passives + 1 worker.
Small flowers 6 passives + 1 worker.
Stems 4 passives + 1 worker.
Triple leaf 4 passives + 1 worker.
Large single leaf 4 passives + 1 worker.

Small single leaf 6 passives + 1 worker.
Basket braids 7 passives + 1 worker.

This pretty basket of flowers has been mounted on a 20 cm (8 in) craft ring which was first covered by working a double crochet all round with the same thread that made the lace.

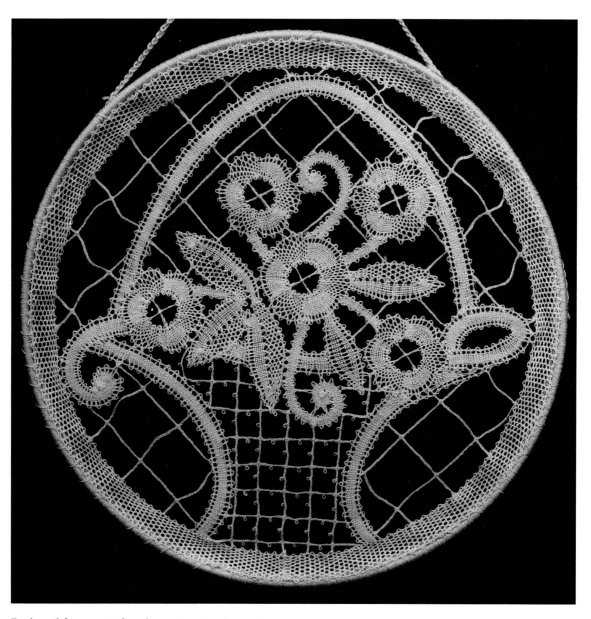

Basket of flowers window decoration (ramhanger)

'Paisley'

Eyelet braid   7 passives + 1 worker.
Other braid   6 passives + 1 worker.
Large flower   10 passives + 1 worker.
Middle flower   9 passives + 1 worker.
Small flower   8 passives + 1 worker.

Here is another asymmetric design with a Paisley origin. It looks equally attractive as a wall or window hanging or framed as a picture. The wide braids are decorated with eyelets. All the shapes with scrolls are started at the scroll. Passive pairs are discarded as they approach the end, where they are sewn in to the beginning scroll.

'Paisley' – an asymmetric design

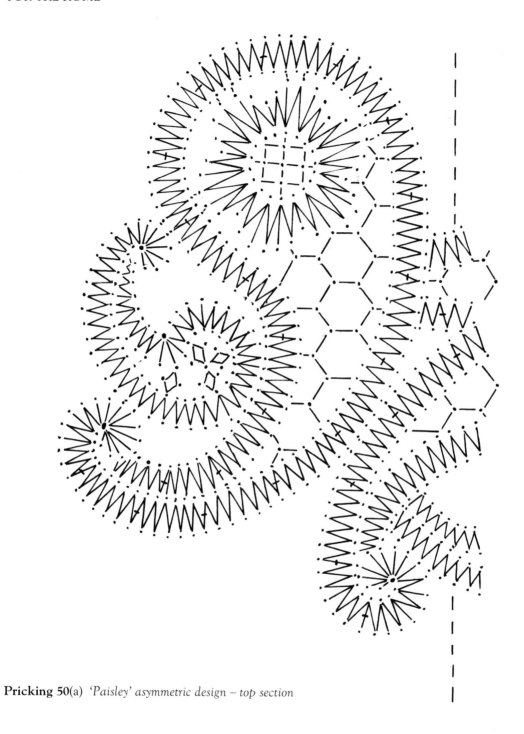

Pricking 50(a) *'Paisley' asymmetric design – top section*

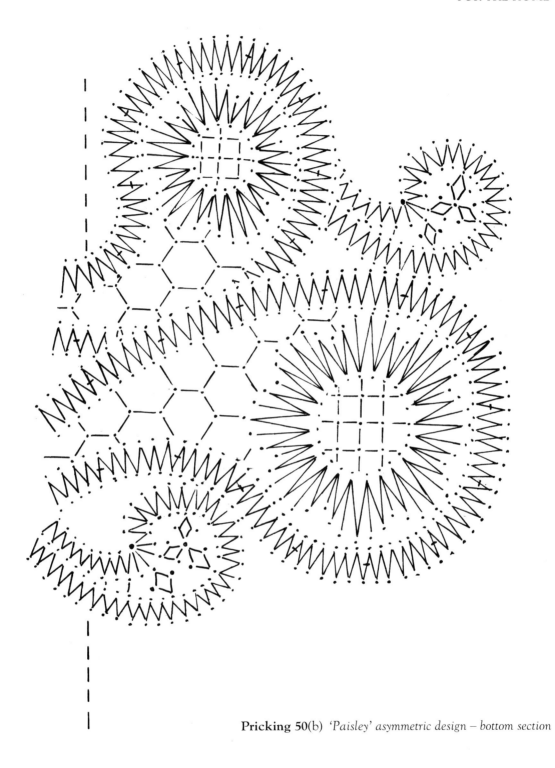

Pricking 50(b) *'Paisley' asymmetric design – bottom section*

Design for a lampshade

Flower 8 passives + 1 worker.
Braid 5 passives + 1 worker.

Each pattern repeat is only joined at one pinhole to the next. This is necessary to give flexibility when mounting: it is very rare to find a lampshade that is perfectly cylindrical. Allowance has to be made for the slope of the shade.

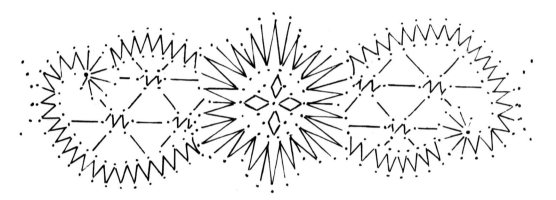

Pricking 51 *Lampshade design – 1 repeat of pricking*

Lace edge on a lampshade

Tray cloth

Centre motif:
Large flower   10 passives + 1 worker.
Centre flower   9 passives + 1 worker.
Braid   6 passives + 1 worker.

Edge:
Large flower   10 passives + 1 worker.
Small flower   6 passives + 1 worker.
Braid   6 passives + 1 worker.

The centre motif can also be used by itself. The straight lines in the filling are a guide for the Torchon ground.

Although the original tray cloth has seven flowers on the longer side and five across the shorter edge, this number can be added to or reduced to fit any other tray. The edge can also be adapted to fit a round tray by altering the relative positions of the flowers and making the edge braid circular.

Tray cloth in the making

Tray cloth finished

Pricking 52(a) *Centre design for traycloth*

Pricking 52(b)
Edge design for traycloth

'Sweetheart' mobile

Flower   11 passives, 1 worker, 1 single wire.
Eyelet braid   9 passives, 1 worker, 2 single wires.
Petalled braid   9 passives, 1 worker, 2 single wires.
Bow: *Eyelet braid*   13 passives + 1 worker.
   Narrow braid   6 passives + 1 worker.

Do not join the different pieces anywhere except at the top.

This free-hanging design requires stiffening, so a single white millinery wire has been used in place of the outer twisted passive pair. It is worked as if it were a gimp thread but it is not wound round a bobbin.

The bow requires no stiffening at all. Work two lengths each of 20 cm (8 in) of *pricking 53a* for the bow and tails and 5 cm (2 in) of *pricking 53b* for the wrapping braid. It is assembled as follows (*diagram 38*):

1   Fold the bow as shown and join the ends, gathering along the centre line at the join.
2   Wrap the narrow braid round this centre line and sew into place. Once again, the ends are joined at the back.
3   Fold the tail braid and slightly gather at the fold. Sew in place at the back of the bow.

Another use for this pretty design is as a gift for a bride to carry with her prayer book or bouquet. The finished lace can be mounted on a silver or gold heart shape.

Note   Although the pricking only shows half of the design, the whole of the flower centre filling is shown because it is not symmetrical about the centre line.

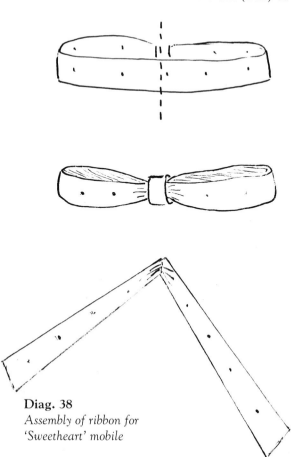

Diag. 38
Assembly of ribbon for 'Sweetheart' mobile

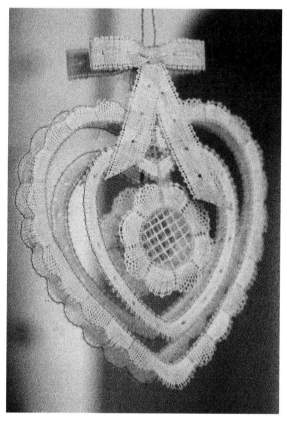

'Sweetheart' mobile

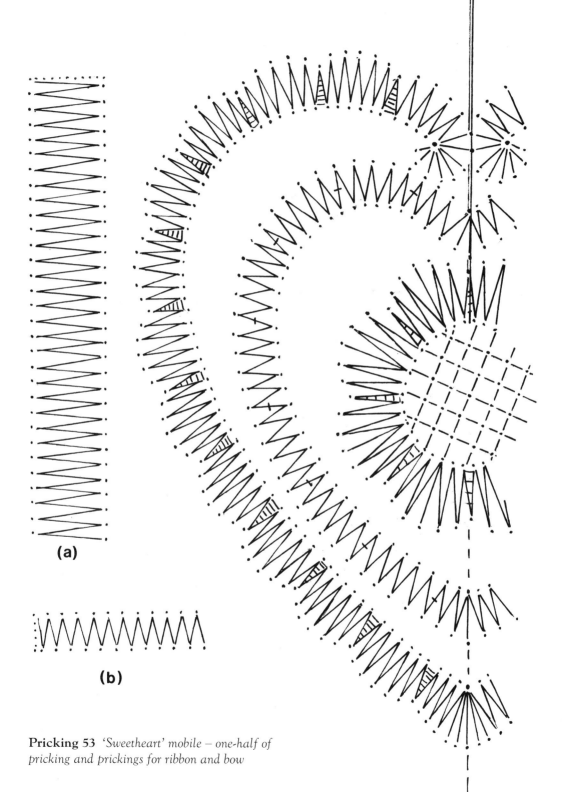

(a)

(b)

Pricking 53 *'Sweetheart' mobile – one-half of pricking and prickings for ribbon and bow*

13
Gifts

It is always a pleasure to make a piece of
lace as a gift. Bruges Flower lace is
especially suitable for this purpose as it
always has a pretty and delicate look, even
when worked in a relatively thick thread.

We offer the designs in this section as
examples of suitable gifts. Some are easy to
work and will take only an evening or two
to make, while others are longer-term
projects.

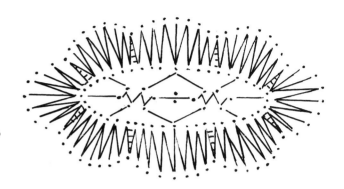

Paper weights

Large design   11 passives + 1 worker.
Small design   7 passives + 1 worker.

Both designs are worked in BOUC 80 Fil de
Lin and fit either oval or oblong
paperweight blanks. They would look
equally attractive mounted on the lid of a
small box or on a greetings card.

Each motif consists of a single oval flower
but the number of petals, size and filling
stitch give them their individuality.

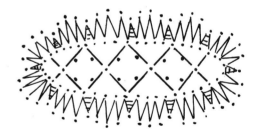

Pricking 54 *Two paperweight motifs*

Paperweight designs

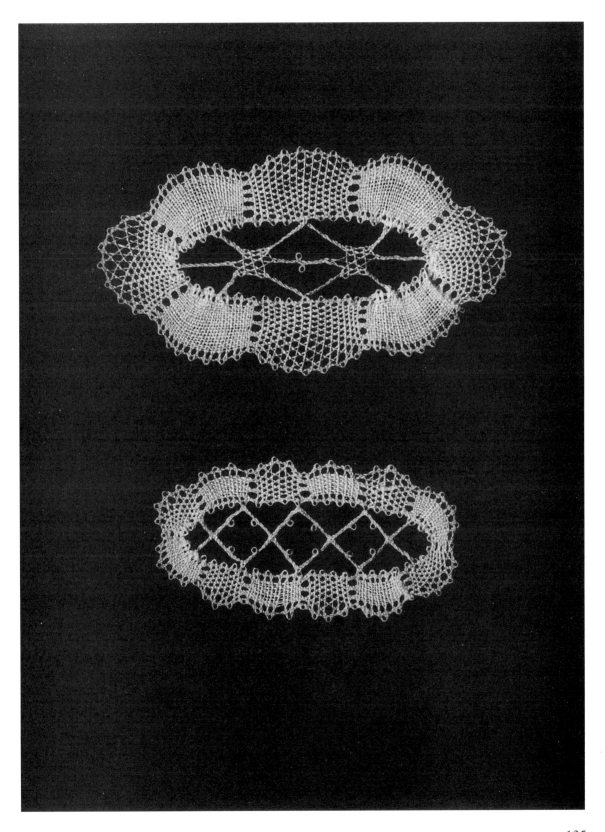

Bookmark

Outer braid 6 passives + 1 worker.
Flower 8 passives + 1 worker.
Inner braid 5 passives + 1 worker.

This design can also be used in a finger plate for a door or as a bell-pull, by working more repeats of the pattern as shown in *diagram 39*. It may be necessary to reduce the size of the pricking to fit a door plate and to use a thinner thread.

The plaited tail is made by winding four thicknesses of thread on each of two pairs of bobbins. These are sewn into the scrolled end before making the plait. The tassel is attached to the end of the plait.

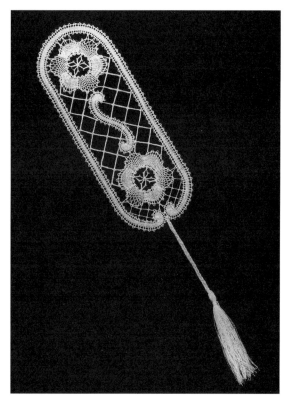

Bookmark

Diag. 39 *Bookmark design showing two pattern repeats*

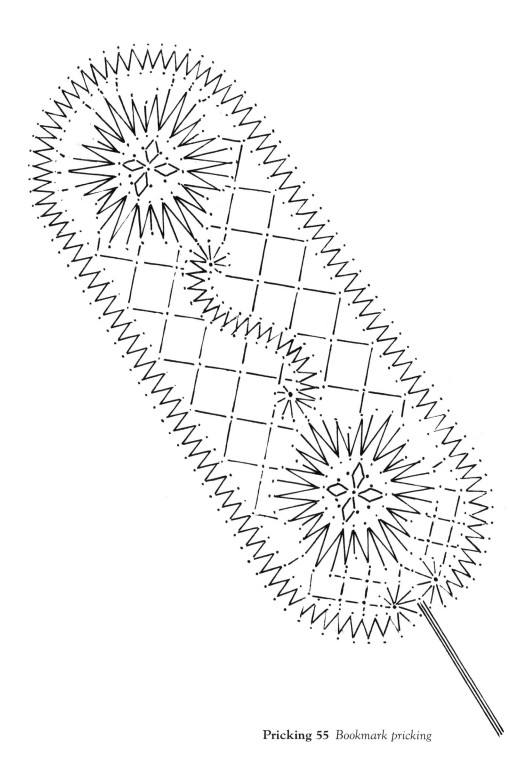

Pricking 55 *Bookmark pricking*

Simple 3-dimensional picture

Large leaf   14 passives + 1 worker.
Middle leaf   12 passives + 1 worker.
Small leaf   8 passives + 1 worker.
Large flower   11 passives + 1 worker.
Middle flower   9 passives + 1 worker.
Small flower   7 passives + 1 worker.

The flowers and leaves are all worked independently. The thread used is thicker than normal and is Bockens 35/2 Swedish linen. The centre vein of each leaf also has millinery wire, to provide stiffness, as passives on either side of the twisted worker. The ends of the leaf threads are bound together with this wire and then wound with florist's tape to form the stem.

The centre of each flower is gathered round a small stamen which has been attached to florist's wire. The threads and wire are then bound with florist's tape to form a stem. No other stiffening is required. If the flowers are worked with the correct tension, they will remain in the correct shape.

The completed flower spray is placed in a 'box' frame lined with dark green felt. It is possible to make more elaborate, larger flower sprays in this manner.

Simple framed 3-dimensional picture

Pricking 56 *Flowers and leaves for the 3-dimensional picture*

Small parasol

'Ribbon' braid   6 passives + 1 worker.
Scroll braid   7 passives + 1 worker.
Flower   8 passives + 1 worker.
Single leaf   9 passives + 1 worker.
Double leaf   4 passives + 1 worker.

The pricking is for $\frac{1}{8}$ of the design. This dainty parasol makes a lovely accessory for a bride to carry, especially if it is lined with the same material as that worn by her bridesmaids.

It fits a frame with 18 cm- (7 in-) long spokes. Many gift shops now sell small Chinese parasols with simple covers that can easily slip off to be replaced with new ones.

Parasol for a bride

If the frame is too small for this design, reduce the pricking and use a finer thread. Conversely, an enlarged pricking requires thicker thread. As an alternative, the centre section as far as the half stitch braid would make a pretty parasol cover by itself (if the frame is small).

Pricking 57
Parasol for a bride – one-eighth of pricking

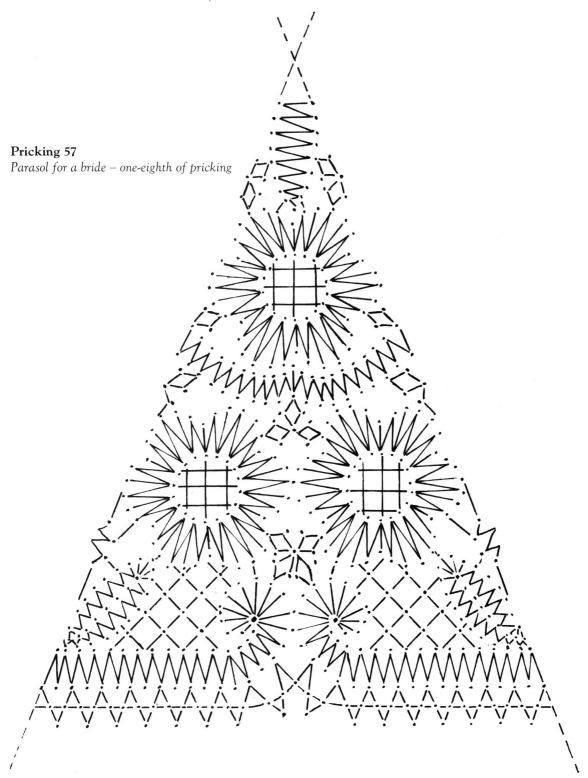

Earrings

Lace earrings can make an unusual present. They are not difficult and can be completed in a couple of evenings.

Three of the designs here are very similar to others in this book but they have been reduced in size and show a variety of interpretations.

By including beads in the lace, extra weight is added, as well as interest. The earring mounts are attached with sewings using the worker pair while the lace is being made. A very light application of fabric stiffener will help the earrings to retain their original shape.

Design No 1 (round flower)

Petals   9 passives + 1 worker.
Inner braid   2 passives + 1 worker.

The inner passives for the braid are replaced with a single thicker thread which is strung with small pearl beads before working. The thread used is DMC 50 Broder Machine.

On the pricking, note that the inner braid has wide distances between the pin holes to leave enough space for the beads.

Design No 2 (oval flower)

Petals   9 passives + 1 worker.

The thread used is DMC 50 Broder Machine. The filling for this design is Torchon ground with beads attached while working it at some of the crossings. The pins are omitted at these places.

Design No 3 (pearl drops)

Braid   5 passives + 1 worker.

The thread used is again DMC 50 Broder Machine. The beads are essential for weight in this design. The pearl drop beads at the base have offset holes, while the string of five beads in the centre is attached during the work. There are left- and right-hand prickings for this and the next design, as they are asymmetric.

Design No 4 (spiral)

Braid   8 passives + 1 worker.

The thread used is BOUC 90 Fil de Lin. Passive pairs are discarded as the braid narrows towards the end. The thread is thicker and therefore heavier than that used for the other earrings and does not require additional beads for weight. It is best to work this design from the centre scroll towards the outside edge.

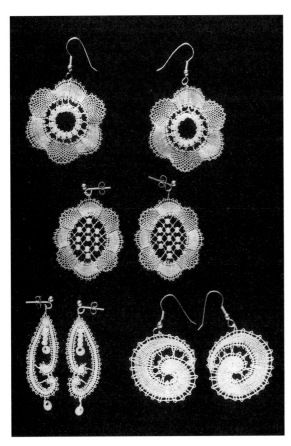

Four pairs of earrings

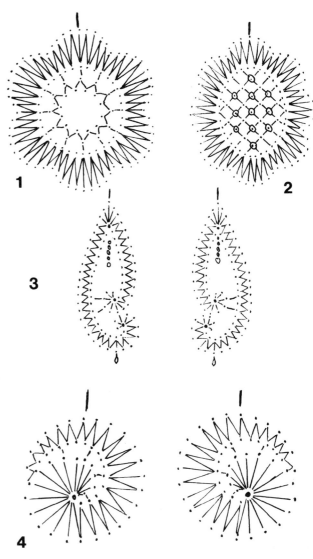

Pricking 58 *Four pairs of earrings*

Lavender/pot pourri sachet

Edge braid   7 passives + 1 worker.
Flower: *Braid*   4 passives + 1 worker.
            Petals   7 passives + 1 worker.

Here is another simple design which is relatively quick to make yet extremely decorative and useful when completed.

The motif has been worked in a lavender-coloured thread mounted on pale-green silk with a small lilac rosebud at each corner and green ribbon for decoration.

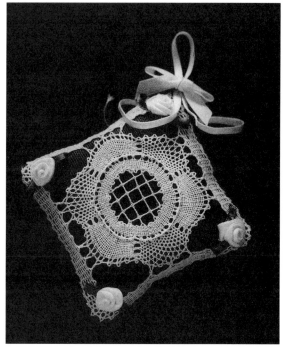

Lavender/pot pourri sachet

Pricking 59 *Pricking for lavender/pot pourri sachet*

Candle frill

Eyelet braid 7 passives + 1 worker.
Outer braid 6 passives + 1 worker.
Scrolled braid 5 passives + 1 worker.

This design consists of basic braids with a
snowflake filling. A total of eighteen pattern
repeats completes the circle, which can be
used in several different ways.

It makes an attractive edge to a mat or it can
be slightly gathered to form a wavy edge for
a smaller mat. By threading narrow ribbon
through the eyelet holes the lace can be
drawn up tightly to form an Elizabethan
ruff which makes a decorative frill round a
candle or its holder. The colour of the
ribbon and thread used can be chosen
either to match or as a contrast to the
colour of the candle.

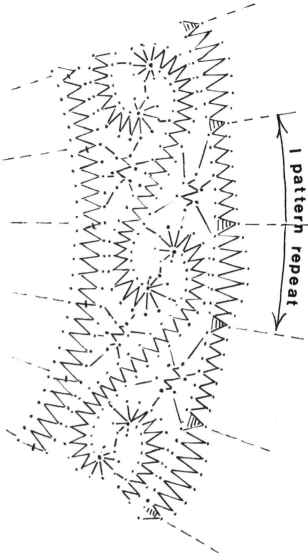

Pricking 60 *Frill for candle holder*

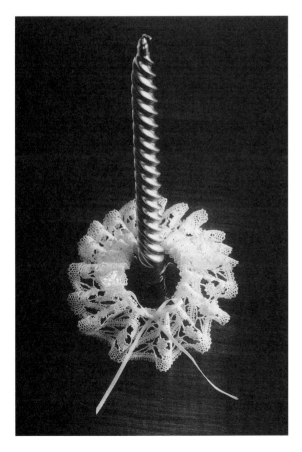

Candle holder with ruff

135

Fan

Outer braid   6 passives + 1 worker and one
    pair in thick gold thread (optional).
Scroll braid   9 passives + 1 worker.
Flower: *Braid*   4 passives + 1 worker.
            Petals   9 passives + 1 worker.

Although traditional Bruges Flower lace
would not use metallic thread, the gold
thread has been used in the edge braid to
echo the gold on the fan sticks.

This is not a difficult design to work but it
is beautiful in its simplicity and reflects the
shapes on the sticks. The Torchon ground
(with three twists) has been used to
complement the decorative cut-out areas on
the sticks, which originated in Spain. A
tourist-type paper/fabric picture was easy to
remove, leaving only the empty sticks.
These fans are readily available in many
countries and are not expensive. They are
made from a plastic material but are pretty
to look at and are sold in a number of
different sizes. Of course, there are also
more expensive wooden and bone sticks
available, or they can be hand-made to
order (see Equipment Suppliers).

Fan

a

b

Pricking 61(b) *Pricking for fan – centre section*

c

Pricking 61(c) *Pricking for fan – right section*

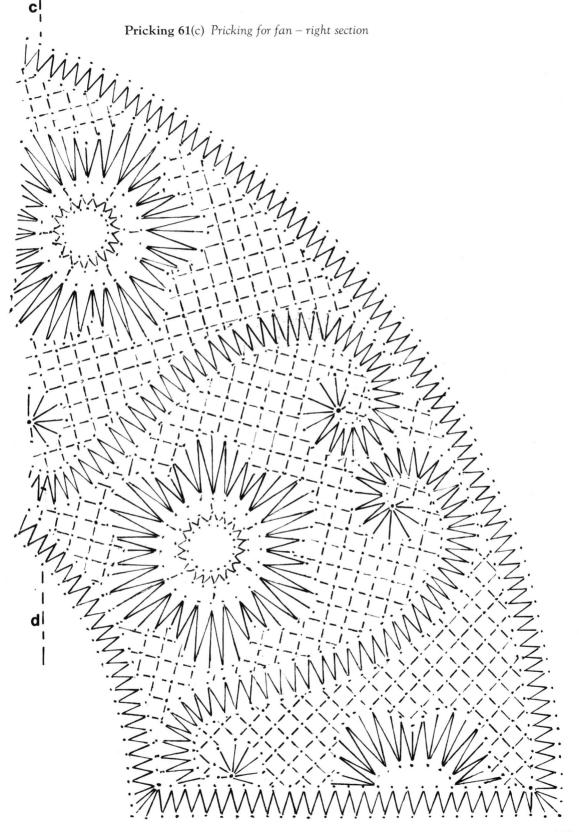

d

Large fan

Once again we can see how versatile Bruges Flower lace is. From the simple design of the previous fan to the complexity of this one, this type of lace can be displayed to advantage.

This fan is unique and was specifically designed for its sticks. It measures some 90 cm (36 in) across with a radius of 45 cm (18 in). It bears a number of entwined motifs, and demonstrates a selection of different fillings and methods of working flowers.

The pricking for this design is not (and never will be) available but it would be relatively easy for a lacemaker/designer who has worked laces from this book to create a similar one (in a required size) which would be similarly unique to its originator.

An interesting addition is the year of design (1989) and the designer's initials (VDS), personalizing the lace. This may be of interest to future historians.

Large fan

Sources of Information

United Kingdom

The Lace Guild
The Hollies
53 Audnam
Stourbridge
West Midlands DY8 4AE

The Lacemakers' Circle
49 Wardwick
Derby DE1 1HY

The Lace Society
Linwood
Stratford Road
Oversley
Alcester
BY9 6PG

The British College of Lace
21 Hillmorton Road
Rugby
CV22 5DF

Ring of Tatters
Miss B. Netherwood
269 Oregon way
Chaddesden
Derby DE2 6UR

United Kingdom Director of
    International Old Lacers
S. Hurst
4 Dollis Road
London N3 1RG

OIDFA

(International Bobbin and Needle
    Lace Organization)

Belgium

OIDFA/Belgische Kantorganisatie
Lydia Thiels-Mertens
Jagersberg 1
B-3294 Molenstede-Diest

France

OIDFA
Suzanne Puech
3 Chemin de Parenty
F-69250 Neuville sur Saône

Germany

OIDFA
Uta Ulrich
Papenbergweg 33
D-4930 Detmold

Deutscher Klöppelverband e.V.
Ortolanweg 7
D-1000 Berlin 47

The Netherlands

OIDFA
Puck Smelter-Hoekstra
Corona 68
NL-3204 CM Spijkenisse

LOKK
Boterbloem 56
NL-7322 GX Apeldoorn

Switzerland

FDS
(Fédération de Dentellières Suisses)
Evelyne Lütolf
Buhnstrasse 12
CH-8052 Zürich

UK

OIDFA
Hilary Booth
39 Craigweil Avenue
Radlett
Herts WD7 7ET

USA

OIDFA
Kathy Kauffmann
1301 Greenwood
Wilmette
Illinois 60091

International Old Lacers
124 West Irvington Place
Denver
CO 80223-1539

Lace & Crafts magazine
3201 Est Lakeshore Drive
Tallahassee
FL 32312-2034

Equipment Suppliers

England

BEDFORDSHIRE
Mrs Sells
Lane Cove
49 Pedley Lane
Clifton
Shefford SG17 5QT

BERKSHIRE
Chrisken Bobbins
26 Cedar Drive
Kingsclere RG15 8TD

BUCKINGHAMSHIRE
J. S. Sear
Lacecraft Supplies
8 Hillview
Sherington MK16 9NJ

Winslow Bobbins
70 Magpie Way
Winslow MK18 3PZ

SMP
4 Garners Close
Chalfont St Peter SL9 0HB

CAMBRIDGEHSIRE
Josie and Jeff Harrison
Walnut Cottage
Winwick
Huntingdon PE17 5PP

Heffers Graphic Shop (*matt coloured transparent adhesive film*)
26 King Street
Cambridge CB1 1LN

Spangles
Carole Morris
Cashburn Lane
Burwell CB5 0ED

CHESHIRE
Lynn Turner
Church Meadow Crafts
7 Woodford Lane
Winsford CW7 1LN

DEVON
Honiton Lace Shop
44 High Street
Honiton EX14 8PJ

DORSET
F. Herring & Sons
27 High West Street
Dorchester DT1 1UP

T. Parker (*mail order, general and bobbins*)
124 Corhampton Road
Boscombe East
Bournemouth BH6 5NZ

ESSEX
Needlework courses
Ann Bartleet
Bucklers Farm
Coggeshall CO6 1SB

GLOUCESTERSHIRE
T. Brown (*bobbins*)
Temple Lane Cottage
Littledean
Cinderford

Chosen Crafts Centre
46 Winchcombe Street
Cheltenham GL52 2ND

HAMPSHIRE
Needlestyle
24–26 West Street
Alresford SO24 9AT

Richard Viney (*bobbins*)
Unit 7
Port Royal Street
Southsea PO5 3UD

ISLE OF WIGHT
Busy Bobbins
Unit 7
Scarrots Lane
Newport
PO30 1JD

KENT
The Handicraft Shop
47 Northgate
Canterbury CT1 1BE

Denis Hornsby
25 Manwood Avenue
Canterbury CT2 7AH

Francis Iles
73 High Street
Rochester ME1 1LX

LANCASHIRE
Malcolm J. Fielding (*bobbins*)
2 Northern Terrace
Moss Lane
Silverdale LA5 0ST

LINCOLNSHIRE
Ken and Pat Schultz
Whynacres
Shepeau Stow
Whaplode Drove
Spalding PE12 0TU

MERSEYSIDE
Hayes & Finch
Head Office & Factory
Hanson Road
Aintree
Liverpool L9 9BP

MIDDLESEX
Redburn Crafts
Squires Garden Centre
Halliford Road
Upper Halliford
Shepperton TW17 8RU

NORFOLK
Stitches and Lace (mail order)
Alby Craft Centre
Cromer Road
Alby
Norwich NR11 7QE

Jane's Pincushions
Taverham Craft Unit 4
Taverham Nursery Centre
Fir Covert Road
Taverham
Norwich NR8 6HT

George Walker
The Corner Shop
Rickinghall, Diss

NORTH HUMBERSIDE
Teazle Embroideries
35 Boothferry Road
Hull

NORTH YORKSHIRE
The Craft House
23 Bar Street
Scarborough YO11 2HT

Stitchery
Finkle Street
Richmond

SOUTH YORKSHIRE
D. H. Shaw
47 Lamor Crescent
Thrushcroft
Rotherham S66 9QD

STAFFORDSHIRE
J. & J. Ford (*mail order and lace days only*)
October Hill
65 Upper Way
Upper Longdon
Rugeley WS16 1QB

SUFFOLK
A. R. Archer (*bobbins*)
The Poplars
Shetland
near Stowmarket IP14 3DE

Mary Collins (*linen by the metre, and made up articles of church linen*)
Church Furnishings
St Andrews Hall
Humber Doucy Lane
Ipswich IP4 3BP

E. & J. Piper (*silk embroidery and lace thread*)
Silverlea
Flax Lane
Glemsford CO10 7RS

SURREY
Needle and Thread
80 High Street
Horsell
Woking GU21 4SZ

Needlestyle
5 The Woolmead
Farnham GU9 7TX

SUSSEX
Southern Handicrafts
20 Kensington Gardens
Brighton BN1 4AC

WARWICKSHIRE
Christine & David Springett
21 Hillmorton Road
Rugby CV22 5DF

WEST MIDLANDS
Framecraft
83 Hamstead Road
Handsworth Wood
Birmingham B2 1JA

The Needlewoman
21 Needles Alley
off New Street
Birmingham B2 5AE

Stitches
Dovehouse Shopping Parade
Warwick Road
Olton, Solihull

WEST YORKSHIRE
Jo Firth
Lace Marketing &
  Needlecraft Supplies
58 Kent Crescent
Lowtown
Pudsey LS28 9EB

Just Lace
Lacemaker Supplies
14 Ashwood Gardens
Gildersome
Leeds LS27 7AS

Sebalace
Waterloo Mills
Howden Road
Silsden BD20 0HA

George White Lacemaking
  Supplies
40 Heath Drive
Boston Spa LS23 6PB

WILTSHIRE
Doreen Campbell (*frames
  and mounts*)
Highcliff
Bremilham Road
Malmesbury SN16 0DQ

Scotland

Christine Riley
53 Barclay Street
Stonehaven
Kincardineshire

Peter & Beverley Scarlett
Strupak
Hill Head
Cold Wells, Ellon
Grampian

Wales

Bryncraft Bobbins
B. J. Phillips
Pantglas
Cellan
Lampeter
Dyfed SA48 8JD

Hilkar Lace Suppliers
33 Mysydd Road
Landore
Swansea

Australia

Australian Lace magazine
P.O. Box 609
Manly
NSW 2095

Dentelles Lace Supplies
c/o Betty Franks
39 Lang Terrace
Northgate 4013
Brisbane
Queensland

The Lacemaker
724a Riversdale Road
Camberwell
Victoria 3124

Spindle and Loom
Arcade 83
Longueville Road
Lane Cove
NSW 2066

Tulis Crafts
201 Avoca Street
Randwick
NSW 2031

Belgium

't Handwerkhuisje
Katelijnestraat 23
8000 Bruges

Kantcentrum
Balstraat 14
8000 Bruges

Manufacture Belge de
  Dentelle
6 Galerie de la Reine
Galeries Royales St Hubert
1000 Bruxelles

Orchidée
Mariastraat 18
8000 Bruges

Ann Thys
't Apostelientje
Balstraat 11
8000 Bruges

France

Centre d'Enseignement à la
  Dentelle du Puy
2 Rue Duguesclin
43000 Le Puy en Velay

A L'Econome
Anne-Marie Deydier
Ecole de Dentelle aux
  Fuseaux
10 rue Paul Chenavard
69001 Lyon

Rougier and Plé
13–15 bd des Filles de
  Calvaire
75003 Paris

Germany

Barbara Fay
Verlag &
  Versandbuchhandlung
Am Goosberg 2
D-W 2330 Gammelby

P. P. Hempel
Ortolanweg 34
1000 Berlin 47

Holland

Blokker's Boektiek
Bronsteeweg 4/4a
2101 AC Heemstede

Theo Brejaart
Dordtselaan 146-148
PO Box 5199
3008 AD Rotterdam

Heikina de Rüyter
Zuiderstraat 1
9693 ER Nieweschans

Magazijn *De Vlijt*
Lijnmarkt 48
Utrecht

Netherlands

Tiny van Donschor
Postbus 482
6000 A1 Weert

Switzerland

Buchhandlung
Dr A. Scheidegger & Co.
  AG
Obere Bahnhofstr. 10A
CH-8901 Affoltern a.A.

Martin Burkhard
Klöppelzubehör
Jurastrasse 7
CH-5300 Turgi

Fadehax
Inh. Irene Solca
4105 Biel-Benken
Basel

New Zealand

Peter McLeavey
P.O. Box 69.007
Auckland 8

USA

Arbor House
22 Arbor Lane
Roslyn Heights
NY 11577

Baltazor Inc.
3262 Severn Avenue
Metairie
LA 7002

Beggars' Lace
P.O. Box 481223
Denver
Colo 80248

Berga Ullman Inc.
P.O. Box 918
North Adams
MA 01247

Happy Hands
3007 S. W. Marshall
Pendleton
Oreg 97180

International Old Lacers Inc.
124 West Irvington Place
Denver
Co 80223-1539

The Lacemaker
23732-G. Bothell Hwy, SE
Bothell
WA 98021

Lace Place de Belgique
800 S. W. 17th Street
Boca Raton
FL 33432

Lacis
3163 Adeline Street
Berkeley
CA 94703

Robin's Bobbins
RTL Box 1736
Mineral Bluff
GA 30559-9736

Robin and Russ
Handweavers
533 North Adams Street
McMinnville
Oreg 97128

The Unique And Art Lace
  Cleaners
5926 Delman Boulevard
St Louis
MO 63112

Unicorn Books
Glimakra Looms 'n Yarns
  Inc.
1304 Scott Street
Petaluma
CA 94954-1181

Van Scriver Bobbin Lace
130 Cascadilla Park
Ithaca
NY 14850

The World in Stitches
82 South Street
Milford
NH 03055